Walking in
Honesty,
Truth &
Integrity

HONOR

KENNETH COPELAND

KENNETH
COPELAND
PUBLICATIONS

Unless otherwise noted, all scripture is from the *King James Version* of the Bible.

Scripture quotations marked *The Amplified Bible* are from *The Amplified Bible, Old Testament* © 1965, 1987 by the Zondervan Corporation. *The Amplified New Testament* © 1958, 1987 by The Lockman Foundation. Used by permission.

Scripture quotations marked *New International Version* are from *The Holy Bible, New International Version*®, © 1973, 1978, 1984 by the International Bible Society. Used by permission of Zondervan Publishing House.

Honor
Walking in Honesty, Truth and Integrity

ISBN-10 1-57562-731-0   30-0053
ISBN-13 978-1-57562-731-1

22 21 20 19 18 17   25 24 23 22 21 20

© 1992 Eagle Mountain International Church Inc. aka
Kenneth Copeland Publications

Kenneth Copeland Publications
Fort Worth, TX 76192-0001

For more information about Kenneth Copeland Ministries, visit kcm.org or call 1-800-600-7395 (U.S. only) or +1-817-852-6000.

CONTENTS

Introduction   5

Chapter 1 The Honorable Life   7

Chapter 2 The Honorless Generation   25

Chapter 3 It's Foolish to Be Honorless   45

Chapter 4 The Honor That Comes From God Only   65

Chapter 5 The Honor Game   79

Chapter 6 Honor and the Covenant   91

Chapter 7 Be Not Slothful in Business   107

Chapter 8 Honor Between God and Man   131

Chapter 9 God Can Make You Honorable   159

INTRODUCTION

In my study of the Word of God, I discovered something very important about honor. *Honor carries and is supported by the supernatural power of God.*

An honorable man may look like a lamb being led to the slaughter. *"As it is* written, For thy sake we are killed all the day long; we are accounted as sheep for the slaughter" (Romans 8:36). He may look like he has just stuck out his chin for someone to hit. He appears this way because he lives by biblical teachings and principles:

"Do unto others as you would have them do unto you." When a man demands your shirt, give him your coat too. Go the extra mile. If someone strikes you on the one cheek, turn to him the other cheek. If your boss doesn't treat you right, honor him anyway. Do the right thing regardless of what it looks like it will cost.

Sometimes it may *look* like we are going to the slaughter when we live according to the Bible definition of honor, but we need to remember what the Bible tells us: that "whatsoever good thing any man doeth, the same shall he receive of the Lord, whether he be bond or free" (Ephesians. 6:8); that "we are more than conquerors through him that loved us" (Romans 8:37); and that the Lord has promised "them that honour me I will honour" (1 Samuel 2:30).

Those are all important principles of godly honor.

If we choose to do the honorable thing—if we choose to live by the Word of God—then the honor of God will hold us up. God will provide for us because of His own personal honor and integrity. He has promised that He will honor us when we honor Him.

In this book we will look at the biblical definition of honor and the results of living an honorable life.

chapter 1

THE HONORABLE LIFE

Simon Peter, a servant and an apostle of Jesus Christ, to them that have obtained like precious faith with us through the righteousness of God and our Saviour Jesus Christ: Grace and peace be multiplied unto you through the knowledge of God, and of Jesus our Lord, according as his divine power hath given unto us all things that pertain unto life and godliness, through the knowledge of him that hath called us to glory and virtue: whereby are given unto us exceeding great and precious promises: that by these ye might be partakers of the divine nature, having escaped the corruption that is in the world through lust (2 Peter 1:1-4).

The Bible teaches honor all the way through even though the word *honor* isn't always used, as in this passage from 2 Peter, which speaks of God's divine nature and His precious promises.

What is honor? The world defines it in many ways, but we will define *honor* as "a keen sense of ethical conduct." Honor is often used to refer to one's word being given as a guarantee. It is personal integrity.

Honor and *honest* are related. They are often used to refer to those who fear the Lord. In many Bible references fear means reverence.

We fear, or reverence, or highly honor God by living life as He directs. God has promised that if we will do that, if we will honor Him and act on His Word, He will honor us (1 Samuel 2:30). A common problem is that many of us have not believed His Word or believed for the blessings promised in His Word.

For instance, we have not understood what Jesus meant when He said for us to turn the other cheek (Matthew 5:39). He was not talking about weakness; He was talking about meekness.

Such scriptures are not referring to our being weak. They are referring to our being submitted to God and committed to doing what He says, whether it looks good to us or not. That is doing the honorable thing.

We must learn to put aside our own feelings and human reasonings and just be obedient to the Lord. Jesus was telling us if we will turn the other cheek in meekness and in the power of the honor of God, we cannot be hit again.

Even though a person turns his other cheek, if he stands on the Word and in the Word, the devil will have a hard time getting through to hit him the second time. In order to do this, however, an individual has to know in whom he has believed. He has to have faith and trust in the honor of God and in His divine integrity.

If you and I know how to walk in honor before God, we don't have to be afraid of anyone. We don't have to fear what men can do to us. The Lord has promised that if we will honor Him and be obedient to His Word, He will honor us and protect us from all our enemies.

Honesty and Honor Go Together

Dearly beloved, I beseech you as strangers and pilgrims, abstain from fleshly lusts, which war against the soul; having your conversation honest among the Gentiles: that, whereas they speak against you as evildoers, they may by your good works, which they shall behold, glorify God in the day of visitation (1 Peter 2:11-12).

Where do we get the word *honest?* If you will study the way this word developed, you will see that it is related to honor. Honor, honesty and truth are closely related concepts.

Peter is saying here, "Let your conversation—your manner of life—be honorable among the gentiles."

Among the Jews of Peter's day the word *gentile* was used to refer to nations or people without God. If you study the book of Ephesians, you will see that at one time you and I were gentiles, but now we who were afar off have been brought near to God by the blood of His Son Jesus Christ (Ephesians 2:13).

This passage is talking about the way we should act toward those who don't know God. Our honorable manner of life, our living honestly among the gentiles, is important. Oh, how important it is.

Let just one or two preachers get in trouble and suddenly all preachers have trouble because of the way a few "Christian" ministers have lived their lives and conducted their business. Instead of walking in honor before the gentiles, these few have disgraced and damaged all believers. We need to understand what God intends for us to do and what we can expect of Him.

Expect of Him? Yes, we expect of Him. If we don't expect something from God when we act on the Word, all we are doing is just making a tradition out of it. We are doing things because someone

said we are supposed to do it instead of because
God said it and we're acting on His Word.

We must learn to walk honestly before the gentiles, so they will behold our good works and glorify
our heavenly Father.

Submit to God-Ordained Authority

Submit yourselves to every ordinance of man for
the Lord's sake: whether it be to the king, as
supreme; or unto governors, as unto them that
are sent by him for the punishment of evildoers,
and for the praise of them that do well. For so
is the will of God, that with well doing ye may
put to silence the ignorance of foolish men:
as free, and not using your liberty for a cloak
of maliciousness, but as the servants of God.
Honour all men. Love the brotherhood. Fear
God. Honour the king (1 Peter 2:13-17).

We are not to use our freedom to hide our shady
dealings. We don't use our power or reputation to
take advantage of someone. We must not use our
position and the respect due us as a preacher of the
gospel or as a child of God to defraud anyone.

Some do, though, and it reflects badly on all of

us—and on the Church of Jesus Christ.

No Discounts, Please!

One time a preacher came into a convenience store where I was shopping. He was trying to talk the clerk into giving him a discount on his shotgun shells because he was a minister. It embarrassed me. It almost made me want to curse so that clerk wouldn't think I was a preacher, too.

I just stood there and shook my head.

The clerk behind the counter got really irritated at the man. He could not have given him a discount, even if he had wanted to, because he did not own the store.

I thought, *My goodness, I can guess what this guy is going to start saying about preachers.*

It doesn't have to be that way, and it shouldn't be that way. The first time I really saw how it should be was while I was a student at Oral Roberts University. Someone told me how Brother Roberts had responded when a barber offered him a discount on his haircut.

"No sir," said Brother Roberts. "I don't accept discounts just because I'm a preacher. I'm not a poor man."

He would not receive it.

"I'll pay the same price as anybody else," he told the barber. "If God puts it in your heart to invest a portion of your income as an offering in this ministry, or any other ministry, that's between you and Him; but I'll pay the full price for my own haircut."

That thrills me. It thrilled that barber, too. He hadn't had many preachers coming in and talking to him like that. Some of them would probably beg him out of his combs if he would give them away.

We are going to have to stop this begging business and dishonorable activity. It is a losing attitude for ministers—and for all believers. It is a bad representation of our Lord. Do you think Jesus would be begging people for a discount? No, no, a thousand times, no!

You never heard Jesus beg. You never heard Him stand up and mock anyone, not even the government. To have biblical honor means to honor and obey the political authorities, even in the face of bad government and poor treatment. You cannot get much worse government and poorer treatment than what was coming out of Rome in Jesus' day.

You never heard Jesus criticize others behind their backs. If He had anything to say about others, He said it to them face to face. Because of that, the Bible says that many of the Jews and Pharisees followed

Him. We tend to focus on the ones who opposed and rejected Him, but the Bible says that many of them did believe on Him and follow Him—in fact, great numbers of them did.

Honor Your Masters

> Servants, be subject to your masters with all fear; not only to the good and gentle, but also to the froward. For this is thankworthy, if a man for conscience toward God endure grief, suffering wrongfully (1 Peter 2:18-19).

The Amplified Bible says verse 17 this way: "Show respect for all men [treat them honorably]."

Servants—employees—be subject to your bosses *with all honor.*

In verse 17 of this chapter we are told to fear God. If you look up the Greek word translated *fear,* you will find that it relates to reverence. We are to reverence the Lord. In the same way, in verse 18 we are told to fear or reverence or give due respect and honor to our masters—our employers.

We know this is true because it is verified in other scriptures. The writings of Paul say the same thing. He wrote to young Timothy: "Let as many servants as are under the yoke count their own masters worthy of all honour, that the name of God and his doctrine be not blasphemed" (1 Timothy 6:1).

Notice that we are to give reverence and honor not only to the good bosses and gentle masters but also to the "froward." The word *froward* means "disobedient or ugly."

Even when our boss is not good, not gentle, not obedient to God, we are to honor him. We are under obligation to treat him with honor and respect, even though he may treat us with dishonor and disrespect.

To do this is "thankworthy." The *New International Version* translates this word as commendable. *Thankworthy* is an old King James English word that is so strong, and so powerful, we need to bring it back into our vocabulary. It is thankworthy if a man, for the sake of conscience toward God, endures grief, suffering wrongfully.

If you will treat with honor a dishonorable boss or superior, you will find favor with God. Of course, you don't have to stay there unless God tells you to, but as long as you work for him, be subject to him. Walk in love. Love never fails. Treat him with honor just as you would if he were good and gentle, even though he is disobedient to God. This is thankworthy, worthy of thanks from God.

In this passage, God is saying to us: "I want to thank you for representing Me there on earth the way I really am, instead of the way the world thinks I am. I want to thank you for looking and acting like Jesus. Don't worry about the one who is abusing or mistreating you. I will take care of him."

God may move you out of that situation, but most likely, you will be an influence on your superior, and you may even win him to the Lord.

It's imperative for you to believe God, and then act like you believe. You must believe and show your honoring of that belief.

Honor Begets Honor

We must honor God by living life as He has directed— every day! This means honoring those above us, being subject to them.

If your superiors mistreat you, crying and moaning won't help. If you keep crying, "They don't like me," then they won't. There really is no reason for them to like you. They don't know God, and you are acting like you don't either.

You are a man or woman of honor. What do you do when someone cheats you out of your vacation or your overtime pay or your rightful promotion? You say: "Lord, You know what's happening here. I'm being treated unjustly. You know it, I know it, and they know it. I just turn this situation over to You. You handle it any way You want."

Then a strange thing will happen: In the end, you will come out ahead. How will that happen? By honoring God, then living in His honor and by your own honesty.

There is nothing that we can't accomplish in honor, in God's honor. There is no place we can't go, no goal we can't reach—if we keep an honorable attitude.

Keep an Honorable Attitude

Christian people can be snobs, though. Some can even be so upright and uptight that they don't live honorably, even when they think they are. I'll give you an example.

I knew a woman in Pensacola, Fla., which is the home of a U.S. naval base with hundreds and hundreds of sailors. When one aircraft carrier docks there, 3,000 people or more may disembark and head to town. Most of the people there know when a carrier or some other large warship has docked.

This dear lady would take tracts with her name and phone number on them and go to every newsstand, pornography shop and tattoo parlor she could find. The first thing she would do would be to open the centerfolds in those girlie magazines and put tracts in them.

Soon after, some sailor would open one of those magazines. He probably had sounded big and tough the night before, but he knew he was just a 19-year-old boy who was a long way from home. No money. No one to call. Nothing to do but look at that magazine. Then he would find that tract right next to the main attraction and call the person whose name was printed on the tract. That is when things would start happening!

This is just the way it happened, time and time again. That woman rescued those young sailors out of sin. She took them home, prayed for them, fed them, took them to church, cleaned them up and sent them back to the Navy as different young men—by the hundreds.

Was she honored for her work? God honored her. But her church kicked her out because somebody saw her coming out of one of those ugly places where she had left her tracts one night.

"Don't you know you're liable to get demon-possessed if you go in there?" she was asked.

"No, I'm not going to get demon-possessed," she answered. "Some little puny demon is not going to run me off—and it ought not run you off either."

Still she was kicked out of the church, so she started her own church. I preached in it. She didn't want to start her own church, but she had to have a place of worship—and she needed a place to bring the sailors.

She was a mother to many servicemen. Some of them would call her and say "I don't have any business looking at those dirty old magazines. I know better than that. I wish you would pray for me. I haven't been acting like I should since I joined the service."

The woman honored God by doing what she was expected to do, instead of acting like a silly, sissy, wimpy, no-faith, dishonorable "Christian." Those sailors were not coming in to the church, so she went out to take the gospel to them and bring them to the Lord. She was kicked out by those who were too upright and uptight to recognize real honor when they saw it.

Through it all, she kept an honorable attitude. She held faith and a good conscience.

Holding Faith and a Good Conscience

This charge I commit unto thee, son Timothy, according to the prophecies which went before on thee, that thou by them mightest war

a good warfare; holding faith, and a good
conscience; which some having put away
concerning faith have made shipwreck: of
whom is Hymenaeus and Alexander; whom
I have delivered unto Satan, that they may
learn not to blaspheme (1 Timothy 1:18-20).

We are to hold faith and a good conscience.

If we put away our faith, we will put away our
conscience. The Apostle Paul tells us that "whatsoever is not of faith is sin" (Romans 14:23).

You may say, "I don't need that faith stuff." Yes, you do.

When somebody announces that he is going to
preach on the faith of God, don't say, "I've heard all
that before." Go hear it again.

Just because you ate breakfast in 1984 doesn't
mean that you don't need to have breakfast today.
You have to eat every morning.

You probably eat the same thing over and over,
day after day, year after year. If you are an oatmeal
eater, imagine how much oatmeal you have eaten.
If you like eggs for breakfast, we would have to line
up chickens from wall to wall to get all the eggs
you have eaten over the last 20 or 30 years. Yet
you don't say, "I don't want to eat eggs; I've already
eaten them once."

You eat the same things again and again. Why? Because the end of proper eating is a healthy body. The end of proper spiritual nourishment is a healthy conscience or spirit man. The end of an honorable life is abundant and eternal life. It comes from living in faith.

Shun Vain Babblings

Study to show thyself approved unto God, a workman that needeth not to be ashamed, rightly dividing the word of truth. But shun profane and vain babblings: for they will increase unto more ungodliness. And their word will eat as doth a canker (one translation says "cancer"): of whom is Hymenaeus and Philetus; who concerning the truth have erred, saying that the resurrection is past already; and overthrow the faith of some. Nevertheless the foundation of God standeth sure, having this seal, The Lord knoweth them that are his. And, Let every one that nameth the name of Christ depart from iniquity (2 Timothy 2:15-19).

In this passage we are told to avoid those who babble all the time, who tell lies, who have their conscience seared to the place that it shipwrecks their lives.

We have seen this take place in all different kinds of ministry and churches. It has come to the attention of the entire world. This kind of thing has been happening in the Body of Christ among charismatic people, among word of faith people, in epidemic proportions. It is an attack of the devil. He intends to destroy us.

Honorable people do not lie.

Vessels of Honor and Dishonor

But in a great house there are not only vessels of gold and of silver, but also of wood and of earth; and some to honour, and some to dishonour (2 Timothy 2:20).

Notice, in a great house there are not only vessels of gold and silver but also of wood and earth. Some to honor, some to dishonor. Which are we? How do we determine which we will be?

A Vessel of Honor

If a man therefore purge himself from these

[faults, sins], he shall be a vessel unto honour, sanctified, and meet for the master's use, and prepared unto every good work. Flee also youthful lusts: but follow righteousness, faith, charity, peace, with them that call on the Lord out of a pure heart (2 Timothy 2:21-22).

How do you become a vessel of honor? By purging yourself. By conducting your life in honor and humility. By fleeing from youthful lusts and following after righteousness, faith, love and peace with all those who call on the Lord out of a pure— and honest—heart.

Honor God, Not the Flesh

Let no man beguile you of your reward in a voluntary humility [or in false humility, telling you that you are no good and so unworthy] and worshipping of angels, intruding into those things which he hath not seen, vainly puffed up by his fleshly mind, and not holding the Head, from which all the body by joints and bands having nourishment ministered, and knit together, increaseth with the increase of God. Wherefore if ye be dead with Christ from the rudiments of the

world, why, as though living in the world, are ye
subject to ordinances, (touch not; taste not; handle not; which all are to perish with the using;)
after the commandments and doctrines of men?
Which things have indeed a show of wisdom in
will-worship, and humility, and neglecting of the
body; not in any honour to the satisfying of the
flesh (Colossians 2:18-23).

Don't honor your flesh. Don't do what your flesh
wants to do. Instead, honor God.

For instance, if you are honoring God, you will
treat your boss like you should—not because it's your
religion, but because it's the honorable thing to do.
You won't act any other way, because you know what
the Word says to do.

When you live by the Word and will of God, you
are living the honorable life.

chapter 2

THE HONORLESS GENERATION

Lord, who shall abide in thy tabernacle? who shall dwell in thy holy hill? He that walketh uprightly, and worketh righteousness, and speaketh the truth in his heart. He that back-biteth not with his tongue, nor doeth evil to his neighbour, nor taketh up a reproach against his neighbour. In whose eyes a vile person is contemned; but he honoureth them that fear the Lord. He that sweareth to his own hurt, and changeth not. He that putteth not out his money to usury, nor taketh reward against the innocent. He that doeth these things shall never be moved (Psalm 15).

Psalm 15 gives us a biblical description of an honorable man. Many have been blessed by knowing such people in their lifetimes.

An Honorable Man

As a young man I understood honor because my father raised me that way. I understood it because both my grandfathers were honorable men; they would rather die than lie. And my grandmothers were honorable women.

I understand what the psalmist means when he writes about the kind of honor "that sweareth to his own hurt, and changeth not" (Psalm 15:4). I understand and respect the kind of person who is going to do the right thing regardless of what it may cost.

My dad lived this way in front of me.

He tithed from the day he and my mother were married in 1927. On their wedding day they made a commitment to one another and to God that they would tithe every dollar God gave them all the days of their married life.

God honored that commitment and supported them through the years. They did not understand many things He tried to teach them because they knew very little about faith. However, the Lord took care of them anyway. During the Great Depression my dad never went 24 hours without a job.

Mother and Dad lived on an old, dry-land farm

in northwest Texas. The only things in abundance there were sand and flies. Yet my daddy had a job because God took care of them.

Eventually, a fellow hired Dad to work in the insurance business. Dad was very successful at it; so just a few weeks after he went with the company, he was moved to Fort Worth as district manager. The man who hired Dad had been planning for a long time to start his own company. He was building up reserves while still working for the company that hired my dad.

But this company had laws, rules and regulations against the sort of thing this man was doing, and some of it was even against the laws of the state of Texas.

This man finally announced he was starting his own company. He had the money and backing to do it, but he needed my father to make it work. He offered Dad a lot of money and a big chunk of the company. He wanted Dad to do for him in the new company exactly what he had been doing under him with the other company. This man based a great deal of his planning on Dad's acceptance of his offer.

It came down to a lawsuit between Dad's company and this man. If they could prove he had done some things wrong, it would cut off over $100,000 from his new company's financing. That was around

1956 when $100,000 was a great deal of money. This man was depending on that money to help establish his new insurance business.

At the trial, my dad was the deciding witness. If the lawyer asked him, "Has this man ever approached you to work for him doing the same job you're doing for your present employers?" and Dad answered no, the case would be closed. The man would get the $100,000 financing, and my father would get a huge chunk of stock and lots of money, along with a high position and much prestige.

If Dad testified that the man had offered him a job with the new company he was planning to start, the man would lose the $100,000 and Dad would get the privilege of keeping his old job.

I was about 19 years old at the time, and was thinking: *Whew, what's Dad going to do? If he takes the stand and answers that question one way, he's an instant multimillionaire.* (The money was already in the till, and the stock was already made out.) *If he answers the other way, all he gets is his old job.*

Wondering what Dad was going to do, I watched as he took the stand. He wasn't a bit nervous or anxious. He didn't have any sweat breaking out on his brow. I couldn't believe he could be so calm.

The lawyer asked the question: "Did this man

offer you a job with his new company doing the same thing that you are doing now?"

Without a second's hesitation Dad answered, "Yes, he did."

When it was over, he stood up and walked away. He left all that money lying on the table and the stock untouched. Later I said, "Boy, Dad, how did you keep from saying what that man wanted you to say?"

"It would have been a lie."

It was as simple as that. To get that money, that stock, that position, Dad would have had to lie. There was never any question in his mind. He just went right on with his business. He gave no more thought to the matter. Every time he would see the man he had testified against, he would walk up, shake his hand and ask how the new company was coming along. That man had such respect for my dad; he loved my dad all his life.

My father is over 80 years old now. His word is still yea or nay. One of the reasons he is so quick to tell the truth is because it is the honorable thing to do. He learned early in life the meaning of honor.

An Honorless Generation

The problem is that this kind of biblical honor is

not being taught and passed down from generation to generation anymore. The young people of today don't hear about it, because it isn't taught to them in our society. Often what they are learning is situation ethics—that right and wrong depend on the situation. This idea sounds right to someone who has not had the honor of God to influence him.

Honor is not taught at home very much either. A child whose sees his father knock his mother across the room or his mother hit his father over the head with a skillet won't know what honor is. He and his future wife will end up doing the same kinds of things.

If a child sees his parents cheating on their taxes or lying to the government or being dishonest with their employers, he will think to himself, *Why should I work my whole life and have nothing when I can get whatever I want by lying?*

He may hear honor preached, but not in church; he'll hear it in street gangs all across the country, as gang members swear honor and allegiance to one another even to the death.

Almost an entire generation has never experienced God's honor and presence because they know virtually nothing about being honorable themselves.

They don't hear biblical honor taught in the Church or in the home. Parents are sending their children to school to learn it, but the schools are not allowed to teach the Bible.

That is why we as parents and believers must take the time to teach honor and integrity to our children.

People Without Honor

Knowing that whatsoever good thing any man doeth, the same shall he receive of the Lord, whether he be bond or free (Ephesians 6:8).

I was raised and trained by parents from two different cultures.

My father is a mixture of Scotch, Irish and English. My mother is Cherokee. Her father was full-blooded Cherokee. The Cherokee people are particularly strong when it comes to raising children. It is traditional for Cherokees to teach their children what they know and how to behave—at home. The European cultural tradition is to train children in everything the parents know, including their trade, education and values, before they are sent away for outside education.

Today, as a rule, honor is not being taught and passed down through the generations, from father to son. Many fathers don't realize that honor requires them to stay with their families and pass along important information to their children.

The honor concept itself is not being passed on from parent to child. That is where this problem in our society began.

This is the reason Crenshaw Christian Center in Los Angeles is rapidly becoming one of the largest churches in the world. I would not be too surprised to see it become the largest. Fred Price, the pastor, is demanding that every man and woman in his church teach biblical honor and the glory of God to their families.

The Bible says that we are to honor our father and our mother (Exodus 20:12; Ephesians 6:1-3). It also requires parents to honor their children by bringing them up in the nurture and admonition of the Lord (Ephesians 6:4).

God has shown me that many people in our society have a real problem with honor. I found out from the Lord that we have an honorless generation on our hands. White, black, brown, yellow, red—all of them are in the same situation. So many of them have no honor. No one has taught them. Their elders have not taught them. No one has lived it before them.

Honor: Requirement, Not Option

I want to show from God's Word some of the reasons why our prayers are not any more powerful than they are. One reason is because our lives are not honorable. Some of the most dishonorable things I have seen in the latter years of my life have come from Christians—Christian teachers and preachers.

We ought to be the world's greatest example of high integrity and the most honorable men and women on the face of God's earth. We must take the time to teach and display honor and integrity to our children; and, if necessary, start all over with them. During the 1960s our society had a dropout generation. At about the same time many of our young people were dropping out, we quit having prayer in school. We took the Name of Jesus and the Bible out of our public school system. Today there is no biblical instruction in American public education.

If a teacher or administrator tries to tell a dishonest or disobedient student that he must be honorable, he may ask: "Why should I? Because you say to? Who are you to tell me how to live my life? My parents fight, lie and cheat—and you're telling me I ought to be honorable?

"You're saying I ought to work my fingers to the bone and learn all this junk you're trying to cram down my throat. What good will it do me to learn all this? I could work another 10 years and still have nothing to show for it. By this time next Friday night I can make all kinds of money by selling drugs to other kids.

"Why should I care if they die? They aren't my kids. You're telling me I should be honorable? Why?"

Unless the adult can pick up a Bible and say "God says so," he can't answer those questions, and he has no right to try. Who are we to tell someone else's child that he ought to be honorable?

The group that dropped out in the 1960s has grown up and produced children of their own. Now we are in the third generation of honorless people.

Today many of the original dropouts have haircuts, wear ties and suits, and some have even become teachers and leaders. Yet some are still doing drugs. Some still have little or no honor themselves even though they've cut their hair and cleaned up, and now they are influencing a new generation of young people.

It's time to go back to the source of honor. It's time to point out the fact that if you do unto others as you would have others do unto you—which is the honorable thing to do—then the honor that comes from God will uphold you.

Even if others mistreat and abuse you, God will support you. They cannot steal from you fast enough to harm you. God will provide for you because of His honor.

God Honors Prayer

Psalm 15:4 says that an honorable person is one who will swear to his own hurt and change not.

We have to live this way again. We have to go back to square one and start all over.

I know one of the finest preachers of the gospel in the United States today. Yet there was a time in his life when he was not serving the Lord. When he came home and found his mother in prayer, he would slam her against the wall and yell, "Shut up that praying!"

But his godly mother would not quit praying. She loved her son despite the way he acted and treated her. Eventually she got him, too. Pistol, blackjack, sticks, stones and all.

Today this man is the sweetest, biggest teddy bear you have ever met in your life. Why? Because that woman of honor would not let go. She lived honorably in front of her son and prayed for him—even with the possibility he might kill her.

This is the kind of stay-with-it, godly person and prayer God honors.

God Honors Covenants

Again I say unto you, That if two of you shall agree on earth as touching any thing that they shall ask, it shall be done for them of my Father which is in heaven (Matthew 18:19).

I want to share with you now about the covenant of marriage between Gloria and me. There are some things that even the minister who pronounced us husband and wife could not do for us. We became one flesh, but there was more to it than that. There was also a mental union and a spiritual union. The preacher could not join us mentally. A mental union cannot be pronounced and produced in 10 minutes. It takes time. So too does a spiritual union before God.

We are married physically. The Word of God says that her body belongs to me, and my body belongs to her (1 Corinthians 7:4-5). We are married sexually. We don't use it, either of us, in bribery or extortion. That is dishonorable.

We also are married mentally. It has taken Gloria time to figure out that I don't think like everybody else. (My mother and father could have told her that!) Actually, most people are that way. We all think and act differently. No two people think exactly alike. Gloria and I had to work at learning to think like each other. As we did so, we started complementing each other. God created us that way, to be one, to be full and strong together, instead of divided and weak in division and despair.

We also have been joined together spiritually. That is something no preacher can do for us. God brought us together. In marriage, there is a miracle action that takes place just as when we are born again. In the new birth, we became one with Jesus. Gloria and I became one with each other when we stood before the minister and were pronounced husband and wife. We agreed to that union. There was a prayer of agreement, a prayer of covenant.

Marriage takes pulling with one another, praying with and for one another. It takes seeking God to find out what we can do to help, support, encourage and understand one another. We have been at it now for over 30 years and because of God's honor between us, it gets sweeter and stronger every day.

There were some things that I did for a long time which just irritated Gloria, and I could not figure out why she was so upset. That still happens occasionally. I can tell when she is irritated about something, but she has too much spiritual sense to throw a fit about it.

We have to be honorable in marriage and in the home. We have to learn honor all over again, and we have to teach it at home. We have to sit down with our children and talk to them about it over and over.

Parents, teachers and pastors must all work together to teach these principles to our children, so they will grow up to be honorable young men and women. Then they will pass on to their children and grandchildren what they have learned from us.

Honor Demands Judgment and Discipline

For if we would judge ourselves, we should not be judged (1 Corinthians 11:31).

Honor demands that we judge ourselves. Many in the Body of Christ are not doing this. Many Christians are waiting for someone else to do the judging. They live with the attitude, "When I get caught, I'll repent!"

There comes a time when each of us needs to judge himself. This scripture says if we will judge ourselves, judgment will not come on us.

Gloria and I are married in the three basic worlds of existence: spirit, soul and body. We are working at and learning about our threefold marriage. She and I are a solid front, especially before our children. Our children have always known that if they come against one of us, they will have to deal with both of us.

We have always stood firm before our children. If I told them, "I'm going to spank you if you do that one more time," and they did it one more time, then the spanking began. Gloria has always supported my decisions and I have supported hers. We have never lied to our children. It is dishonorable to lie to a child—to tell him you are going to do something and then not do it.

It is also dishonorable to spank a child for every little thing he does wrong. Punishment should be suited to the offense.

When I was growing up, a spanking was a major event in our house, a serious incident. We would carry on and on about it. It was a big deal. My father had to travel in his work and when he came home and took charge of the situation, it was a serious occasion. But it was not done dishonorably. We would talk about what I had done and why I was being punished. We would sit down and discuss the wrongdoing and the consequences, then I got what was coming.

Our son John came in one day and asked his

mother, "Mama, do they send five-year-old boys to jail?"

When your child asks a question like that, you know immediately something is wrong. It turned out that he had set the grass on fire. An entire vacant lot was burned. Fire trucks and flashing lights were everywhere. It scared the daylights out of him! He was worried about what was going to happen when I got home.

"Do we have to tell Daddy?" he wanted to know.

"Yes," his mother assured him, "we have to tell your daddy."

I think he would rather have gone to jail.

When I got home Gloria said, "John has something to tell you." He came in and told me what he had done. I guess he figured I was going to unload on him right there, just bend him out of shape. Instead we sat down and had a family discussion.

I said, "John, I was present one time when they dragged two little charred bodies out of an old garage and put them in body bags. That's all those little boys' daddy had left. I want you to know right now that I'm not going to go through life without you. I'm not willing. And you won't ever forget this."

We talked and talked and talked. Then I did several things to reinforce the point I was trying to make—that's been over 20 years ago and he hasn't forgotten it yet!

The Bible does not say spare the rod and spoil the child. This is the secular interpretation of Proverbs 13:24 which actually says, "He that spareth his rod hateth his son: but he that loveth him chasteneth him betimes."

The rod is not just a stick. It is any type of honorable correction. The Bible also says, "Withhold not correction from the child: for if thou beatest [spank, not abuse] him with the rod, he shall not die" (Proverbs 23:13). It is an honorable thing to teach our children and to discipline them according to the Word of God.

Dishonor Hinders God's Blessings

Likewise, ye husbands, dwell with them according to knowledge, giving honour unto the wife, as unto the weaker vessel, and as being heirs together of the grace of life; that your prayers be not hindered (1 Peter 3:7).

Right now we are in the midst of one of the mightiest outpourings of God's blessings in the history of mankind. Yet many believers are missing out on these blessings. The Apostle Peter tells us that prayers are hindered because of dishonorable lives. This applies not just to husbands, but also to wives and children.

Honor is an integral part of prayer—and vice versa. Prayer doesn't work for someone who is continually disobedient to the Word of God. If one claims to be a child of the living God, but at the same time is mistreating one of His children, then that person cannot expect God's blessing to continually be on his prayer life.

As husbands and wives, as brothers and sisters in Christ, we have a covenant agreement before God as well as a covenant agreement with one another. I must be just as honorable to the Body of Christ as I am to my wife and to my God. You are His child just as much as I am. How can I be dishonorable to His child and at the same time be honorable to Him? It can't be done, because you are bone of His bone and flesh of His flesh.

Honor Pleases the Lord

I have no greater joy than to hear that my children walk in truth (3 John 4).

When we honor one another because of obedience to the Word—not because of tradition, not because of our own selves, but because of God's command—the Lord is very pleased. It is the godly thing to do.

Jesus Christ of Nazareth has honored us with His Name and His life. When we act on that kind of honor and walk in it, when we are honorable regardless of our feelings or our finances or whatever else we think we might lose if we do so, we are truly walking hand in hand with Jesus.

Walking in truth, honesty and honor pleases our heavenly Father.

chapter 3

IT'S FOOLISH TO BE HONORLESS

As snow in summer, and as rain in harvest, so honour is not seemly for a fool (Proverbs 26:1).

For the turning away of the simple shall slay them, and the prosperity of fools shall destroy them (Proverbs 1:32).

A fool and honor are like oil and water—they do not mix. The Bible does not say that prosperity ruins a person. It says it ruins the fool. The key to this situation is, don't be a fool.

How do you know you are not a fool unless you go to the Bible and find out what a fool is? One thing we know already about a fool is that he is dishonorable. He does not know the honor of God.

Honor does not look right to a fool. It just makes no sense to him.

We have been "blessed" in recent years with an

outstanding work of foolishness called situation ethics. If there ever was a concept imbued with the life of a fool, it's situation ethics.

Basically, situation ethics says that right isn't always right and wrong isn't always wrong—it depends on the circumstances or the situation. It is really an excuse to be dishonorable. I guarantee you, the person who thought up this theory does not really believe it himself. It seems right, however, to anyone who does not have the honor of God inside him to influence his thinking.

Recently, I was praying over a situation that had to do with a young, born-again man who had gotten into some serious trouble. Everybody around him was totally shocked by what he had done. They knew he had committed his life to God and the ministry. There was no question about it.

The worst thing about the whole situation was how he felt about what he had done. He could not understand that he had done wrong.

When I heard about it, I prayed, "What's the matter with him? Has he taken leave of his senses?"

No, the Lord answered, *he's dishonorable. You have a whole generation of honorless people. They don't know anything about honor.*

There are such people in all segments of society

today. We see them everywhere. In every area of life there are dishonorable men and women. Even our ministers and spiritual leaders are not immune to dishonor, as we have seen all too often.

We must always be on our guard lest we too fall prey to the devil's devices. We must be careful to keep our eyes on the Lord and our feet on the path of honor.

The Picture of Honor

Wherefore seeing we also are compassed about with so great a cloud of witnesses, let us lay aside every weight, and the sin which doth so easily beset us, and let us run with patience the race that is set before us, looking unto Jesus the author and finisher of our faith; who for the joy that was set before him endured the cross, despising the shame, and is set down at the right hand of the throne of God (Hebrews 12:1-2).

The greatest picture of honor is Jesus in the Garden of Gethsemane. He could have called forth 12 legions of angels to set Him free, but He did not (Matthew 26:53-54). He had every right to do so, but He knew if He did that, we would go to hell. Later, at Calvary, He withstood the shame and the pain that was put upon Him for the joy that was set before Him. This was honor.

We are to look to Jesus, the author and finisher of our faith, as our example of how to lead honorable lives in the midst of a crooked and perverse generation.

Back to the Basics

We have to teach and preach honor just as if our generation had never heard of it—because many of them have not!

We have to return to the fundamentals of personal integrity and Christian responsibility. We have to teach once more the most simple principles, such as: When you use something that belongs to somebody else, wash it, clean it, fill it with gas or fix it (even if you didn't break it) before you return it. Whatever you borrow, return it in better condition than when you got it.

Here is another of the most basic principles of honor: Don't lie. The most dishonorable thing you can do is to misrepresent or distort the truth.

"But, Brother Copeland, Christians don't lie."

Sure, they do. Just because you and I are believers does not mean that we are not part of today's dishonest society. Let me give you an example.

"We're having a meeting at the church Thursday night. Are you coming?"

"I'll sure try to make it."

Often that is a pure lie. The person has no intention of coming. It is obvious that he does not plan to attend, or he would not have said "try to make it." He is just leaving himself an opening, a way out. That isn't the Christian thing to do.

Believers ought to not have an escape hatch. Jesus taught us to make our word either yes or no. He said that all else proceeds from evil (Matthew 5:37).

I know all this is really basic; but when you get to the fundamentals of honor, you get down to the heart of God. He is truth!

Don't Be Foolish

For so is the will of God, that with well doing ye may put to silence the ignorance of foolish men (1 Peter 2:15).

It is the will of God that by our honorable lives we put to silence foolish men. So who are foolish men? Solomon said honor is as unseemly to a fool as snow is in the summer. So dishonorable men are foolish men. We are not to be foolish, but wise. Honor is a sign of true biblical wisdom.

We Are Beloved, Honorable Sons

Moreover I will endeavour that ye may be able after my decease to have these things always in remembrance. For we have not followed cunningly devised fables, when we made known unto you the power and coming of our Lord Jesus Christ, but were eyewitnesses of his majesty. For he received from God the Father honour and glory, when there came such a voice to him from the excellent glory, This is my beloved Son, in whom I am well pleased (2 Peter 1:15-17).

Peter wrote to the believers of his day: "After I depart I want you to remember what I told you. We are not following cunningly devised fables, because we were there as eyewitnesses with the Lord Jesus when He received *honor* and glory."

In our daily lives, you and I are to reflect the same honor and glory that was bestowed upon Jesus by God. By doing so, we too are pleasing to our heavenly Father, who has promised to uphold us just as He upheld Jesus.

Honor One Another

Be kindly affectioned one to another with brotherly love; in honour preferring one another; not slothful in business; fervent in spirit; serving the Lord; rejoicing in hope; patient in tribulation; continuing instant in prayer; distributing to the necessity of saints; given to hospitality (Romans 12:10-13).

In this passage, the Apostle Paul tells us how we are to act in our relationships with our fellow Christians. We are to love one another, care for one another, be patient with one another, pray for one another and honor one another. We are not to get involved in situation ethics.

Situation ethics is typically for people who are so-called "basically honest." This means they do not lie unless they are under pressure or when it is to their advantage. This is not honor.

Honor and Dishonor

Therefore thou art inexcusable, O man, whosoever thou art that judgest: for wherein thou judgest another, thou condemnest thyself; for thou that judgest doest the same things. But we are sure that the judgment of God is according to truth against them which commit such things. And thinkest thou this, O man, that judgest them which do such things, and doest the same, that thou shalt escape the judgment of God? (Romans 2:1-3).

Here Paul is talking about people who judge, including those who sit on the bench.

This passage is true for anyone who takes it upon himself to sit in judgment of another person, whether he is a duly authorized court judge, pastor of a church or a father or mother over a family. In the eyes of God the only true judge is one who is appointed and ordained by Him. You and I have no business judging anyone.

If a criminal was brought up before me, and I was told, "Judge this man," I would have to say, "I can't; I don't have the authority and power to judge him." I could pronounce all kinds of judgment against him, but it would not mean a thing. Nobody would carry out my judgment. If anyone did, he would be as much a criminal as I or as the man I had judged.

We do not have the right to pass judgment on our

fellow human beings made in the image of God.

Why then do we address a judge as "your honor"? Because he has been given the awesome authority and power to exercise legal dominion over the lives of other men and women.

What is that authority and power called? *Honor.* And it is a recognizable honor. Doesn't that fit the pattern of honor? This authority and power is given to him to execute judgment that is written (Psalm 149:9).

Now, what about a judge who is dishonorable? First, we must recognize that this is a contradiction in terms. Let's see why.

What is dishonor? According to the Bible, if you give a person honor, you have given him dominion. You have given him authority. When that individual is dishonorable, he uses his authority and power to his own advantage—to better his own life, to increase his own power, prestige and position, to line his own pockets. He is using honor in a dishonorable manner.

A soldier, for example, is given the authority and power to carry a weapon. That is an honor. His government has entrusted him with a firearm. His country has bestowed upon him the right to use it against the enemy. For him to use that weapon for his own purposes or designs is wrong. What happens to such a person? He is dishonorably discharged from the service for misusing the dominion that was given him.

That is what Paul is talking about in Romans 2:1. Literally he is saying that the one who passes judgment on his neighbor is trying to clear his own conscience before God by being quick to condemn another person for the same offense he is guilty of himself.

Now let's see how this applies to our daily lives. There is not much that you and I can do about a dishonorable county, state or federal judge—except to vote and pray, believing God for a solution to the situation. And don't underestimate the power of prayer.

Similarly let's take the Supreme Court as an example. You and I may feel that some Supreme Court justices have been dishonorable; but we cannot vote them out, because we did not vote them in. We can, however, pray them out.

I have been part of that. I have heard the Lord say to me in my prayer time, *Pray this way.*

"Why?" I asked. "What are we doing here?"

His answer was, *I'm going to change the Supreme Court. I'm going to change that situation,* He told me. *There are certain things I want you to pray. Most of it you will have to pray in the Spirit, because you do not know what to pray for as you ought. Besides that, you have no business knowing much about the man.*

That kind of thing is between God and the person

in question. But we can pray the way God tells us, and He will take care of the situation for us.

This applies to the Church, and particularly the ministry. Listen to God and watch the situation so you can pray as you should—not so you can condemn, but so you can pray.

For instance, you may be told to pray for some preacher who is always criticizing women. He gets in the pulpit and preaches about their hair, their face, their clothes, their attitude and their actions.

He may start out preaching about the Resurrection, but the first thing you know, he is preaching about short skirts. He can't seem to get off the subject of women. Watch out for such a man. It may be that he is trying to save his own spirit, trying to salve over his own conscience. It is likely that he is either chasing women or wanting to badly. He may even be into pornography, and it has a hold on him. So, it comes out in judgment. That isn't always the case but many times it is.

When a person comes down on men and women of faith, it is often a sign that something is wrong with him on the inside. If the truth were known, you would find jealousy. You would find a person who has very little faith. He knows it and is embarrassed about it, so he tries to cover up and excuse it every way he can. Then judgment starts to come out in his life. What is that? Dishonor.

That man is using a position of honor in the wrong manner. He needs our prayers.

That is what I meant when I said a dishonorable judge is a contradiction in terms. The same is true of a dishonorable Christian, whether a minister or not. Each of these individuals by definition is a person of honor. For one of them to act in a dishonorable manner is contradictory. This is what Paul is telling us in Romans 2.

Honor—The Key to Life

Or despisest thou the riches of his goodness and forbearance and longsuffering; not knowing that the goodness of God leadeth thee to repentance? But after thy hardness and impenitent heart treasurest up unto thyself wrath against the day of wrath and revelation of the righteous judgment of God; who will render to every man according to his deeds: to them who by patient continuance in well doing seek for glory and honour and immortality, eternal life (Romans 2:4-7).

Notice that Paul again brings honor into his

discussion. He brings up judgment to teach about honor. In this passage he was writing to the born-again Church, who did not know about honor. He repeatedly wrote about honor because the Church knew nothing about it.

To our own disadvantage, we have not paid nearly enough attention to honor. If we had, those of us who are old enough to have lived when honor was taught would not be wondering why it has become so rare.

If we had given it the proper attention, we would have taught it to and practiced it in front of our young people. Then they wouldn't seem to know so little about it.

One of the principals of the high school I attended was a man of honor. He wouldn't let me drop out of school. By rights he should have just kicked me out, considering some of the stunts I pulled. But this man of honor would not let me drift away. He had a standard and he lived it in front of me. He taught me honor.

In Colossians 2:23 Paul says that we are not to honor ourselves to the satisfying of the flesh. That means we don't give our flesh authority or dominion. We don't honor it by just letting it do whatever feels good. This will lead to lasciviousness and it will destroy you. But honor will lead to life.

Honor—Delegation of Authority and Dominion

God created the heavens and the earth. He owns them and has dominion over them. I cannot give you dominion over the heavens and the earth. I can tell you about it, but I cannot give it to you. It is not mine to give.

As chief executive officer of Kenneth Copeland Ministries, I have authority, and I can delegate my authority. Any time I delegate my authority to someone, I am telling that person he is honorable. I want that person to act in my best interests.

If I delegate to a dishonorable person, he will use his authority to steal. If I bring in a dishonorable man, honor him and put rank on his shoulders, he will steal from me.

If he is an honorable man, however, he will use that dominion and authority for the betterment of the community. It is a straightforward, simple principle.

Some men seek authority and dominion so they will have the opportunity to steal. Government at all levels has many such people. They are exposed in the newspapers all the time.

Even a morally minded, honorable man who gets in one of those high-class, high-ranking, high-pressure jobs will be tempted to do things he swore he would never do.

Real honor comes from the Spirit of the living God. The determination and power to stand in honor—to do what is right—even when it looks like it will destroy you *comes from Him.* That kind of strength comes from God, from knowing Him. That kind of wisdom comes from His Word. The Bible says very plainly that in the right hand of wisdom is length of days, and in her left hand are riches and honor (Proverbs 3:16).

To honor someone, you have to delegate authority to that person. To honor your father and mother, you have to delegate authority over your own life to them. An honorable parent will exercise proper authority and dominion over his children as they submit to him—and a dishonorable parent will not. An honorable boss will exercise proper authority over his employees as they submit to him—and a dishonorable boss will not.

Honor and Submission

I beseech you therefore, brethren, by the mercies

of God, that ye present your bodies a living sacrifice, holy, acceptable unto God, which is your reasonable service (Romans 12:1).

The Bible says that humility must come before honor (Proverbs 15:33). For me to honor God, I must give Him authority over my thinking. Doesn't the Bible tell us in Romans 12:1 to offer our flesh (our bodies) as a living sacrifice, which is our reasonable service? In this same chapter the Apostle Paul begins his discourse on Christian order in the Body of Christ.

To honor God, I must also give Him dominion over my thought life. I must give Him dominion over my flesh, instead of just doing whatever I feel like doing. If I don't, it's lasciviousness—one of the most cancerous sins that exists. It will eat your life away from the inside out.

If you practice lasciviousness (or complete indulgence) in any area of your life, you will lose your restraint in other areas. You will become accustomed to practicing lawlessness. If you lose your honor, if you stop acting in honor toward others, you are on your way to self-destruction. Lasciviousness will destroy you physically, mentally and financially—and it will destroy your witness. You can be pastor of the largest church in town, but without honor you will fail.

God gave man dominion over all the works of His hands. He honored him when He gave him dominion over all the earth. But what did man do? He dishonored God. He honored Satan by giving him dominion over himself. Adam honored the devil and made him lord and master, and he didn't do it out of ignorance. The Bible says that the Eve was deceived, but the man, Adam, was not (1 Timothy 2:14). He went into this sin with his eyes wide open. He committed high treason against God and brought dishonor to the authority and dominion God had bestowed upon him.

Honor comes from the delegation of authority and dominion. Remember, the Scripture says honor your father and your mother (Exodus 20:12). Do you realize what that is telling you to do? Give your father and mother authority over yourself. Give them dominion. Submit to them. It does not mean just to talk nice about them in public. That is man's idea of honor.

"Oh, doesn't he honor his mother? He always has his arm around her."

But he won't do anything she tells him to do.

That is man's counterfeit of honor, the kind of honor people pass around to one another. The honor of God is the delegation of authority and dominion. It is bowing the knee before your father and your mother as a little child and doing as you are told. Honor is when you are not afraid to say: "I'm sorry, guys, I can't do that. My mother and father don't allow it."

"What difference does that make?"

It makes a big difference. It shows that you have yielded authority and dominion to them. Oh, we have lost so much in this area. This really needs to be said over and over.

We have trained our young people to be dishonorable to a great degree because we have been so hell-bent on them attending college and becoming a success. (I'm using these strong words because they are right.) We have been so hell-bent on advancing their careers that we have neglected their character.

Why? So they can make more money. We have fostered this make-all-the-money-you-can idea and then encouraged our children to go out and "find" their own identity.

Learning From Parents and God

I discovered that I did not need to find my identity. I needed to learn what my father, A.W. Copeland, knew.

At one time I rebelled against him. I dishonored him. I didn't give him authority over me. Oh, up to a point, I did. I gave him authority and dominion while I was in his presence. But when I got out of his sight, I did whatever I wanted to do.

The things that my father taught me and practiced in front of me were for my benefit. They were honorable things. I finally came to the point where I realized I was being stupid. I was out trying to learn things the hard way that my father already knew. I realized I could learn them from him and not have to pay the price of learning them for myself.

I came to understand that I could start my own life of learning after I had learned what my father knew—and I could get his years of experience free of charge and in a whole lot less time than it took him to learn it.

The reason some children of successful men and women are not worth much is that they don't bother to learn what their parents know about building a life or a business. In some cases, their parents fail to instill it in them. Often, children set out to learn for themselves rather than let the Lord teach them.

I found out when I went to college that if I didn't learn from God, I wasn't going to learn a thing in college. I came to see that honor was the answer—honoring God, honoring His Word and putting it first place in my life. Please don't take me wrong. I am not underestimating the value of a college education.

But if what a person learns at the university does not conform to the principles of God and His honor, then it is not an education. It is really just a head full of nonsense—useless facts and procedures.

Wisdom Will Put You Over

Happy is the man that findeth wisdom, and the man that getteth understanding. For the merchandise of it is better than the merchandise of silver, and the gain thereof than fine gold. She is more precious than rubies: and all the things thou canst desire are not to be compared unto her. Length of days is in her right hand; and in her left hand riches and honour (Proverbs 3:13-16).

It is not knowledge that will put you over the top—it is wisdom.

Wisdom is the God-given gift to know what to do with knowledge. Wisdom gives understanding. There is in God a *wisdom* understanding of honor.

When you have a godly understanding of honor, it takes away the fear of acting on it. In the next chapter, we will learn more about the kind of honor that comes only from God.

chapter 4

THE HONOR THAT COMES FROM GOD ONLY

I have greater witness than that of John: for the works which the Father hath given me to finish, the same works that I do, bear witness of me, that the Father hath sent me. And the Father himself, which hath sent me, hath borne witness of me. Ye have neither heard his voice at any time, nor seen his shape. And ye have not his word abiding in you: for whom he hath sent, him ye believe not. Search the scriptures; for in them ye think ye have eternal life: and they are they which testify of me. And ye will not come to me, that ye might have life. I receive not honour from men (John 5:36-41).

Honor that comes only from God is very special. This is the kind of honor Jesus was referring to here in John 5. He was talking to the Jews who had censured Him not only for doing the works that He did, but also for doing them on the wrong day of the week.

Think how horrible it must be to heal a man on the Sabbath. That's just terrible, isn't it? No, of course it isn't! God had said, "Remember the sabbath day, to keep it holy" (Exodus 20:8). I wonder what those Pharisees thought healing was—unholy? That's how twisted the minds of men can get.

Jesus told them that the Father Himself had sent Him and bore witness of Him, but that they did not even know Him because they did not have His Word abiding in them. This must have been a terrible shock to the self-righteous Pharisees. They spent a lot of time reading the Scriptures and felt very confident in their own understanding.

"You are looking in the Word, searching for eternal life," Jesus said, "and here I am. The very Scriptures you are studying testify of Me."

He went on to tell them: "You say you are searching for life, but you won't come to Me that you might have life. I don't receive honor from any of you."

That is a terrible indictment to make about anyone, that he does not give honor to the Son of the living God.

The Honor of Men

But I know you, that ye have not the love of God in you. I am come in my Father's name, and ye receive me not: if another shall come in his own name, him ye will receive. How can ye believe, which receive honour one of another, and seek not the honour that cometh from God only? (John 5:42-44).

Here is the honor that comes from God only. By coming to Jesus, instead of going away from Him as these Pharisees were doing, we learn God's definition of honor from the Bible.

Man's definition of honor is a derivative of the honor of God, but it is light and shallow. There is no depth to it. It is almost dishonorable in view of what some men do to get it.

Let's take the military, for example. One man is honored by rank. He is given honor because he has proven to be a leader of men. The longer and better he does his job, the more promotions to higher rank he receives. Finally he is promoted to general. Rank has privilege. It has honor. This man has come to his high position honorably. Men stand in awe of this officer, and they should.

However, some men who wear the marks of high rank get them dishonorably—by scheming, begging or doing favors to gain approval. The only reason they want rank is so they can walk in money and pride and throw their weight around. That is not honor; it is dishonor.

Such men are a discredit to the uniform they wear. They are a particular discredit to those who have led men into battle and won their badges of rank honorably.

The schemers have the same rank, the same "honor," the same privilege, as those who deserve them—but they did not come by them honorably. They achieved man's honor—man's way.

Let's look at Psalm 8. It will help us understand the kind of honor that comes from God only.

The Honor of God

O Lord our Lord, how excellent is thy name in all the earth! who hast set thy glory above the heavens. Out of the mouth of babes and sucklings hast thou ordained strength because of thine enemies, that thou mightest still the enemy and the avenger. When I consider thy

heavens, the work of thy fingers, the moon
and the stars, which thou hast ordained; what
is man, that thou art mindful of him? and the
son of man, that thou visitest him? For thou
hast made him a little lower than the angels
(Hebrew: "God"), and hast crowned him with
glory and honour. Thou madest him to have
dominion over the works of thy hands; thou
hast put all things under his feet (Psalm 8:1-6).

This is the Bible definition of honor. God has given
us honor and dominion over the things that are His.

The Honor of Jesus' Name

But God has honored us in an even more important way: He has given us the honor of His Son,
Jesus. And Jesus honored us even more by giving us
the use and authority of His Name.

After Jesus was raised from the dead He said to His
disciples: "All power, all authority, has been given
unto Me both in heaven and in earth. Therefore, you
go into all the earth. Take My Name and cast out Satan. Lay hands on the sick, and they will recover. Do
it in My Name" (Matthew 28:18-19; Mark 16:15-18).

Jesus gave us authority and dominion over Satan,

sickness and disease. He also gave us authority over spiritual communication. We have every right to pray in the spirit.

What did He do? He honored the Church with His Name, His blood, His covenant with God. He gave us dominion over all the forces of darkness because He gave us His Name.

With what else could He honor us? What more could we possibly want or need?

Eternal life? He has honored us with everlasting life when we were born again (John 3:16).

His presence? He promised never to leave us nor forsake us (Hebrews 13:5).

His own person? He made us bone of His bone, flesh of His flesh, spirit of His Spirit (Ephesians 5:30; 1 Corinthians 6:17).

His love? He loved us so much that He gave Himself for us (Titus 2:14).

You cannot honor a person any more than by giving your whole self.

Crowned With Honor

O Lord our Lord, how excellent is thy name in all the earth!...hast thou ordained strength.... and hast crowned him with glory and honour (Psalm 8:1-2, 5).

Crowned with glory and honor.

Here the psalmist is talking about praise, power and dominion, about the Name of God and His glory.

"How excellent is Your Name. How powerful is Your Name. How filled with authority is Your Name."

He is talking, too, about God having given man dominion over all the works of His hands. Isn't that an honor? Certainly. It is an honor that could have come only from God. He's the only One with the authority to give dominion over what belonged to Him.

Honor Carries Authority

And God blessed them, and God said unto them, Be fruitful, and multiply, and replenish the earth, and subdue it: and have dominion over the fish of the sea, and over the fowl of the air, and over every living thing that moveth upon the earth (Genesis 1:28).

In Genesis 1, God created the heavens and the earth. He created Adam and gave him a will of his own. God gave him His faith and His life. He created Adam to think His thoughts after Him. God breathed into him the breath of life, and Adam became a living soul.

His mind and emotions came alive (Genesis 2:7).

Where would Adam have gotten any thoughts if not from God?

He had God's mind and God's thoughts in him. Then God honored him. The glory of God covered him. He crowned him (Psalm 8:5). Who wears a crown? A king—one in authority.

God delegated to man authority over all the earth, and it filled Satan with envy and jealousy. He wanted the authority God had given to man so he set out to steal from Adam what God had rightfully bestowed on him. You know the story, how Satan tempted mankind into disobeying God. By doing so, man lost to Satan what God had given to him. He lost glory. He lost the honor. He lost the power to enforce authority and dominion.

Satan was Lucifer, the anointed cherub, before he fell from heaven (Ezekiel 28:14). He had been honored with command over all of heaven's praise and glorious music. He was an archangel who had command over at least one-third of the heavenly host (Revelation 12:3-4, 9). But he wanted more; and God had given what he wanted to man.

When Satan made his move to rob Adam, instead of standing firm and obeying God, Adam went along with his wife. To do that, he had to bow his knee to

Satan. It was a dishonorable act.

Adam dishonored the authority and dominion God had given him. By doing so, he took off the crown God had honored him with and placed it on the head of Satan and bowed down before him. Later, Satan said to Jesus: "See all these nations and their glory? I will give them to You if You will bow down before me. They have been given to me. They are mine, and I can give them to whomever I will" (Luke 4:5-7).

Where did Satan get that authority and dominion? From Adam. How was Adam able to do that? Because they were his to give. They had been given to him by God Himself. God had honored him.

It was a dishonorable act on the part of man. He really did not own the earth enough to give it away, but authority had been delegated to him. And God honored his decision. God did not back down from His Word to Adam. He would not be dishonorable and demand that the crown of authority and dominion He had given to man be returned.

Today, because of what man has done with his God-given authority and dominion, God has had to continue to honor certain things where Satan is concerned. Why? Because God is not dishonorable.

God took an honorless, evil, lawbreaking, truth-twisting being and defeated him on man's level—and

He did it honorably. He did it without breaking the law of heaven or of earth. He did it without breaking His Word. He confirmed it on Resurrection Day when Jesus said: "All power has been given to Me, both in heaven and on earth. Therefore, you go into all the earth, and in My Name cast out the devil. Lay hands on the sick, and they shall recover." (See Matthew 28:18; Mark 16:15, 17-18.)

Once Jesus had redeemed the crown from Satan, He immediately used it to crown His Church—the Body of Christ. He crowned us with honor, glory and dominion.

In Ephesians 6:13 we are told to take on the full armor of God. What is the Lord doing? He is delegating authority, endowing us with the honor that comes from God only.

The honor that only God can give is dominion and authority in the realm of the spirit. How did He convey that honor upon us? How did He bestow upon His Body, the Church, dominion and authority in the realm of the spirit?

Think about what God has given us the authority to do, to receive and to put under our feet. He has given us authority in His Word. He is no respecter of persons (Acts 10:34). That means that the promises God has made in His Word, He has made to each of us.

He has given us authority over our physical body and over the curse of the law. We are redeemed from the curse. We have been endowed with power and authority over Satan and his demons. We are honored with the very clothing of war that Jesus wore when He defeated all the enemies of hell—the full armor of *God*.

The Whole Armor of God

And the Lord saw it, and it displeased him that there was no judgment. And he saw that there was no man, and wondered that there was no intercessor: therefore his arm brought salvation unto him; and his righteousness, it sustained him. For he put on righteousness as a breastplate, and an helmet of salvation upon his head; and he put on the garments of vengeance for clothing, and was clad with zeal as a cloak (Isaiah 59:15-17).

Isn't this also listed in Ephesians 6:11-17? The Bible says we are to take on the whole armor of God. And do what? "Be strong in the Lord, and in the power of his might" (Ephesians 6:10).

The Lord has delegated to us authority, and He

has honored us with the right and privilege to wear his fighting armor. He has given us the right and authority and privilege to have His nature, to have His mind, to receive and be filled with His Spirit, to speak His Word, to use His Name to do His works.

The love of God has been shed abroad in our hearts by the Holy Ghost (Romans 5:5). Think about that. Think about the capacity that has been given to us as spirit beings so that we are able to house the love of God Himself—the love that never fails.

To where does all this point? To the blood-covenant relationship we have in Jesus through which God has called us His own (Hebrews 2:11-12). We are His family. Do we see that? Do we know that? Both God and Satan know it.

God's "Untouchables"

We know that whosoever is born of God sinneth not; but he that is begotten of God keepeth himself, and that wicked one toucheth him not (1 John 5:18).

...Touch not mine anointed, and do my prophets no harm (1 Chronicles 16:22).

We are "the untouchables." When we keep ourselves in the Lord, the evil one cannot touch us. God warns Satan, "Keep your hands off what is Mine."

To walk in that anointing, that place of divine safety and security, we have to watch ourselves. We have to keep ourselves walking the love walk. If we step off that path, Satan can get a shot at us.

God has honored you and me as only He can. He has delegated to us authority that only He possesses. He has given us dominion over what is His. We have received honor that comes from God only.

chapter 5

THE HONOR GAME

We have explored the kind of honor that comes only from God. In doing so, we looked at John 5.

I want us to take another look at that same passage of scripture, so we can better understand man's honor, or the "honor game" as I call it. To do so, we will go further back, to John 5:15. This will help set the stage for what Jesus is saying.

Prideful Men Won't Accept Jesus

The man departed, and told the Jews that it was Jesus, which had made him whole. And therefore did the Jews persecute Jesus, and sought to slay him, because he had done these things on the sabbath day. But Jesus answered them, My Father worketh hitherto, and I work. Therefore the Jews sought the more to kill him, because he not only had broken the sabbath, but said also that God was his Father, making himself equal with God (John 5:15-18).

The Pharisees wanted to kill Jesus. He had healed a man on the Sabbath day, and had said God was His Father. They were so filled with pride and envy, they refused to accept Him as God's Anointed.

Jesus Receives No Honor From Men

As we have already seen in John 5:37-38, Jesus rebuked the self-righteous Jews for their stubbornness, pride and unbelief. He said to them:

Ye have neither heard [the Father's] voice at any time, nor seen his shape. And ye have not his word abiding in you: for whom he hath sent, him ye believe not.

He tells them in verses 39-40 that they read the Scriptures trying to find eternal life, but refuse to come to Him that they might have it. He says:

Search the scriptures; for in them ye think ye have eternal life: and they are they which testify of me. And ye will not come to me, that ye might have life.

Then in verse 41 He goes on to say, "I receive not honour from men." He does not mean that He refuses honor. He means, "God is the One honoring Me, not men. If you want to honor God and His Word, you must come to Me."

Jesus Refused to Play the Honor Game

But I know you, that ye have not the love of God in you. I am come in my Father's name, and ye receive me not: if another shall come in his own name, him ye will receive (John 5:42-43).

In these passages, Jesus is pointing out to these men that He will not play their honor game.

What's the honor game? Giving each other "honor" or medals or titles in order to boost one's own sense of self-worth. I'll give you rank so you can give me privilege, etc. That is pride and greed, not honor.

Jesus is not saying that men should not honor other men, because the Word of God says we should give honor to whom honor is due (Romans 13:7). It is a wonderful thing to honor the hard work and diligence of other men. It is, however, a dishonor to God to seek the honor of others rather than that which comes only from the Lord.

You and I cannot demand that we be given honor. For instance, we must not demand that others call us "doctor" or "teacher" or "master." This is the very thing Jesus is talking about to the proud Pharisees of His day—and to us in our day.

Jesus won't play honor games.

Seek God's Honor

How can ye believe, which receive honour one of another, and seek not the honour that cometh from God only? (John 5:44).

Notice the word "only" at the end of this sentence. As we have discovered, there is honor that comes *from God only.* You cannot give it to me, and I cannot give it to you. I can only tell you about it.

For instance, I cannot give you the kind of honor that conveys authority over the devil. I can tell you about your authority over Satan, but it is God who has given that authority to you. How did He give it to you? By giving you His Name.

I cannot give you God's Name. I could give you my name and enter into some kind of covenant agreement with you. I could adopt you, thereby bestowing my family name upon you; but that act would not give

you authority over the devil. It might give you authority over my earthly possessions, but not over the
enemy of your soul.

Only God can give you that power and dominion. Why? Because only His Name has authority over
the evil one. That is an honor that only God can give.
Jesus spoke about this honor in a passage of Scripture
from Mark's Gospel.

A Prophet Without Honor

And he went out from thence, and came into
his own country; and his disciples follow him.
And when the sabbath day was come, he began to teach in the synagogue: and many hearing him were astonished, saying, From whence
hath this man these things? and what wisdom
is this which is given unto him, that even such
mighty works are wrought by his hands? Is not
this the carpenter, the son of Mary, the brother
of James, and Joses, and of Judah, and Simon?
and are not his sisters here with us? And they
were offended at him. But Jesus said unto
them, A prophet is not without honour, but in
his own country, and among his own kin, and
in his own house. And he could there do no

mighty work, save that he laid his hands upon a few sick folk, and healed them. And he marveled because of their unbelief (Mark 6:1-6).

Jesus said that a prophet has no honor in his own hometown.

When He went back to Nazareth where He had grown up, He found that there was certainly no honor for His ministry or for God. The total lack of honor and appreciation in the people of that city meant that He could do no mighty works there because of their unbelief.

To believe God, then, is to honor God. Jesus said to the Jews, "If anyone honors Me, he honors the One who sent Me" (John 5:23). When He said that a prophet is without honor in his own land, and that He received honor from no man, He was not saying He refused to receive honor from men. He was saying He did not receive the honor of men because none was being offered. There is a big difference between the two.

He was referring to the fact that many of the people of His own area did not come to Him to honor God or His ministry. In fact, they dishonored God by refusing to believe the Word that Jesus preached.

Receiving Honor of Men Rather Than of God

> But I know you, that ye have not the love of God
> in you. I am come in my Father's name, and ye
> receive me not: if another shall come in his own
> name, him ye will receive. How can ye believe,
> which receive honour one of another, and seek
> not the honour that cometh from God only?
> (John 5:42-44).

These men were playing the honor game with
each other. That is why they would not recognize
Jesus for who He was and render to Him the honor
due Him as a prophet of God. They chose their own
honor rather than that which comes from God only.

Honor that comes from God only is something
that belongs to God. It does not belong to men.

Jesus was talking about all the aspects of God's honor
that we discussed in the last chapter—power over
the devil, power over our bodies, spiritual communication, eternal life, etc. God is the source of all these
honors. I could preach to you about receiving them
and promise them to you, but they can only come
from Jesus. He has been given all authority in heaven
and earth.

I have the honor and the authority that comes from God to minister to you, to tell you about the honor and to allow His gifts and honors to flow through my spirit, and even at times through my hands. Yet, they do not come *from* me, but from Him.

Counterfeit Honor

Another part of the honor game is using counterfeit honor instead of the real thing. Counterfeit honor is false honor—nothing but pride.

Did you ever hear someone say, "I'm a man of honor; our family fights for its honor"? He is not fighting for honor, but for pride—the kind of honor that once was used to justify two men dueling at daybreak because of a supposedly insulting remark.

Today, that kind of honor will provoke one person to attack another because he doesn't ride the same kind of motorcycle—or maybe because he does. It will cause gangs of young people to square off against one another. They get in the middle of a vacant lot or even on a crowded street with chains, knives, bats and guns just because someone is found on the wrong turf.

That's not honor. That's the pride of a fool. It's the counterfeit of the real thing and it's deadly.

If you recognize that as counterfeit honor, if you know from where it comes, you can take the negative side of it, flip it over and recognize the real thing.

Communicating True Honor

Since the real nature of honor has largely gone untaught, caring and knowledgeable Christians have fought an uphill battle. Far too many of us have been trying to teach honor using religion as the basis. The concept of honor has become lost in the translation. Many people today have no foundation for receiving spiritual teaching.

Part of this problem is that the Church is divided into so many different denominations, associations and affiliations that we no longer speak the same language. Through the years we have developed different vocabularies as well as different doctrines and practices. The result is that we have different terminologies for different things.

Various groups of Christians speak different languages. They speak the language of Protestant, Catholic, Evangelical, Fundamentalist, Pentecostal and on and on.

To effectively teach honor—real honor—to someone else, we must learn to speak his language. We have to learn to interpret our message in terms that he can understand. We must base the teaching we are trying to impart to him on something he knows.

Let me give you an example.

Not too long ago, I heard a street gang member being interviewed on television. He was asked if he would kill.

"Yeah," he answered.

He was asked what would cause him to kill. Immediately he responded, "If somebody jumped on one of my boys, I'd do what I gotta do."

My ears perked up.

"Did you hear that, Gloria?" I exclaimed. "There's a covenant between those kids, and they're honoring their covenant."

If somebody would go into those gangs, preach the blood of Jesus and talk with those young people on a basis they understood, we would see some results. He might ask them: "Did you know that Jesus is offering Himself as leader of your group, your gang, your family of people? His message is simple. He's saying: 'You come to Me. When the devil jumps on you, I'll do what I have to do. I'll give you My weapons. I have given you My life.'"

Believe me, they would understand that type of language.

When I preached the blood covenant this way in Africa, some of those people sat on the edge of their seats. And they didn't stay there! They jumped out onto the floor. I was talking about the foundation of their culture—their life.

When I began to talk to those people about honor coupled with that kind of covenant, I presented the gospel in a way they could understand. In their culture they would rather die than dishonor a covenant. They would rather give up their lives than criticize or curse somebody who is in covenant with their family. It is a matter of honor. In fact, these people are taught that they will die if they dishonor a covenant.

Covenant Honor

Look at the old covenant sometime to find out how dishonorable people fared. A man who dishonored his family was put to death. That got their attention! That kind of thing will make people fairly honorable whether they want to be or not.

In the new covenant, our honor comes from God, who not only watches over us but dwells within us. Our honor comes from within. If we will act in honor, then the power of honor within us will support and sustain us, regardless of whether or not we seem vulnerable to others. Being vulnerable has no bearing on it. If we only are honorable when we are not vulnerable, we are into situation ethics or situation honor.

Being honorable only as long as it is to our advantage is not honor at all. A person who regularly practices situation honor will usually decide at some point that practicing any honor any time is too expensive. He will soon lose his honor.

When we lose our honor, even if it's in just a few situations, we lose the preciousness of life. It is really even worse than that. The things we do are eternal. We live with them forever. We need to look at everything we do that way.

Do you realize that if we adhere to God's Word and treat our brethren with honor, preferring one another, we will rarely have to make a decision? It has been made for us. There is no question about the "right" thing to do.

I don't have to decide whether I want to speak to you again. You don't have to wonder how you should relate to me. We don't have to stop and think how we are supposed to treat one another. It is already decided. We are already committed to it. The decisions are already made for us.

Living by God's Word, His code of honor, is the simplest way to live on the face of the earth. Why do we fight it so?

chapter 6

HONOR AND THE COVENANT

By humility and the fear of the Lord are riches,
and honour, and life (Proverbs 22:4).

The Bible, literally, is a book about covenants.
Both the Old and New Testaments have honor as the
primary point of focus. Honor is central to all the
other principles of the Bible.

It is very interesting that we find so much about
honor and the covenant in Proverbs. This entire book
concerns the godly teachings of a wise man who is
instructing his son how to live a righteous life.

The Bible says God chose to establish His covenant with Abraham because He knew Abraham
would teach his children to "keep the way of the
Lord"; that is, to live a life based upon and filled with
honor for God (Genesis 18:17-19). To do so is to be
in right-standing with God.

Right-Standing With God

He that followeth after righteousness and
mercy findeth life, righteousness, and honour
(Proverbs 21:21).

Jesus echoed these same words in the New
Testament when He said, "Seek ye first the kingdom
of God, and his righteousness; and all these things
shall be added unto you" (Matthew 6:33).

He told us to seek not after the things of this
world, but after God and right-standing with Him.*
He promised that if we would do so, all the things we
need would be added to us.

Proverbs 21:21 is in the same light. It assures us
that anyone who follows, or seeks, after mercy and
right-standing with God will receive both with honor.

Now, most Bible interpretations of the word *mercy*
give a false impression of its real meaning.

I will try to explain. Before we can talk about
mercy, we have to look at some other words as well.

Remember, the Bible is a book of covenants. Both
the Old Covenant and the New Covenant were written to people who understood the meaning and

---

*Note that when we become believers in Jesus Christ, we are the righteousness of God Himself.
(Second Corinthians 5:21 tells us that God made Jesus, who knew no sin, to be sin for us that
we might be made the righteousness of God in Him.) The word *righteousness* translated literally
means to be "in right-standing." When a man accepts Jesus, he moves into a position of new
birth. He is put in right-standing with God.

significance of a covenant relationship.

English translators have used the word *testament* in place of *covenant*. The word testament really refers to the will or desires of a person to be carried out after his death. That is why this word was chosen rather than *covenant*. The English translators were showing that the New Testament is the "Last Will and Testament" of Jesus. When He died for us, we inherited His Word, His promises.

The word *testament,* however, does not really match the original Hebrew. It loses the most important concept. The Hebrew word translated "covenant" is *beriyth* and means "...cutting...; a compact (...made by passing between pieces of flesh)."[1] It refers to a cut made in the flesh so that blood flows as evidence of a binding agreement between two parties.

A covenant is more than a contract or a promise. It is the most binding agreement in existence, because blood is involved. It is more serious, more formal, more permanent, because it involves a blood relationship.

The word *mercy* is similar to *testament.* It is a weak translation of a very powerful concept.

A rendering of the Greek word *agape* in the New

---

[1] James Strong, *Strong's Exhaustive Concordance of the Bible* (Nashville: Abingdon, 1890), "Hebrew and Chaldee Dictionary," p. 24, #1285.

Covenant is translated "love," "mercy" or "compassion." But this really has a passive or inactive connotation or meaning. The concept of mercy can best be described by the words "will love." Now, that is powerful.

In essence, the person who enters into a covenant relationship with another is saying to him, "I swear in blood that I will love you forever." It has nothing to do with what the other person does or does not do. It is an oath of love. It is not in return for favors. It is forever, regardless.

The Hebrew equivalent of the Greek word *agape* is *hesed*. It literally refers to the compulsion to give and to love without limit those who have no merit. That is why, in the New Testament, the English translators sometimes used the word *charity*.

Somehow, the concept did not come across. There is so much giving involved in mercy that our English words don't really convey the full implication or significance.

This concept is best seen in a covenant. The strongest covenant we know of is that which exists between Jesus and the Church. In essence, Jesus said: "I am giving Myself to you. That includes everything I have and everything I ever will have. Everything that is Mine is yours. You have My Name, My Word and My nature. Anyone who comes against you comes against Me. Anybody who curses you curses Me. Any enemy of yours is My enemy as well. When you are assailed, just call upon Me and I will do whatever I must to guard, protect and rescue you."

That is mercy.

Keep this concept in mind because it affects the word *honor.*

Proverbs 21:21 could be translated: "He who seeks after right-standing with God—anyone who has a blood covenant with Him—finds life, righteousness and honor."

Giving Life to Gain Life

Give, give, give—not take, take, take. That's the way we must live. In order to give, we have to make ourselves vulnerable. That's what Jesus did. He made Himself vulnerable when He gave Himself for us.

Losing sight of ourselves will cause us to find life.

Remember how Jesus put it? "He that findeth his life shall lose it: and he that loseth his life for my sake shall find it" (Matthew 10:39). The man who seeks to keep his life will eventually lose it, but he who gives up his life for the sake of Jesus and His kingdom will find it.

The person who gives will find life, dominion,

authority—*and honor*. When he gives his life, or puts it at risk, when he makes himself vulnerable obeying the Word of God, he places himself in a position in which God can trust him with dominion, authority, riches, life—and what else? Honor.

Honor Brings Responsibility

But if an individual is dishonorable, he will be unable to handle the dominion, authority, riches and honor that come upon him. Instead, he will allow them to handle him. Soon, he will honor the gifts rather than the Giver. God will not allow that to go on for long. It is not part of the covenant, the blood-sworn contract between God and His people.

A minister friend of mine named Tommy Tyson said it best. He heard a word from the Lord and described it like this: "Oh, it blessed me. Here came the miracle I was praying for. But after the miracle came the responsibility of what to do with the miracle. If you have a miracle outpouring of souls coming into the kingdom of God, you're going to be responsible for those little spiritual babies. You're going to have to handle that miracle. That's when the hard work comes in. You can't just walk away and wash your hands of it."

Honor When No One's Looking

Love your enemies, bless them that curse you, do good to them that hate you, and pray for them which despitefully use you, and persecute you (Matthew 5:44).

Therefore all things whatsoever ye would that men should do to you, do ye even so to them: for this is the law and the prophets (Matthew 7:12).

An honorable man is one who is the same whether anybody's looking or not. He is honorable to his boss whether he is liked or not. He is honorable to the company whether he is treated right or wrong.

That is the honorable man. He acts as if there is no one around but him and God. He acts the way his covenant or contract calls for him to act. He acts honorably.

Imagine that I am working for you and you are that hateful boss. I am in God's covenant with you. There is a blood covenant in Jesus' blood that has brought us together and made us one. I must honor you and prefer you. If you continue to misuse and abuse me, I don't have to stay in your employment unless the Lord says to, but as long as I am there I must work for you in honor, treating you as if you were Jesus Himself, never dishonoring you in word or deed.

Jesus said we are to love those who misuse and persecute us. He was talking about the power of honor. When He said do unto others, He did not say do unto others *before* they do unto you. He said do unto others the way you want them to do unto you. The way we deal with others is the same way with which we will be dealt.

As we walk in God's honor, we are to prefer one another (even those who persecute us) and not follow our flesh or the thoughts in our mind. Eventually, the majority of people will treat us the same way in return. Why? Because God honors His promises. If you and I keep our part of the covenant, God will see to it that others do so as well. They will live in honor toward us.

We are in a blood covenant relationship with Almighty God. Our name is His Name, and His Name is our name (Deuteronomy 28:10). We are one. We must represent our namesake the way we desire Him to represent us.

This covenant relationship is very real to me. It's as real as if I had taken a knife, cut open my hand to let blood flow, thrust it into the bleeding side of

Jesus and said, "I covenant with You forever." But my blood would have been a disgrace to His blood. His blood was not tainted with sin. I didn't need to mix my blood with His. His blood took the place of my blood.

When I plead the blood of Jesus Christ, Satan hears that plea. He knows that I know what I'm talking about. My enemies have become God's enemies. That blood is a covenant between me and the Almighty. When any Christian begins pleading the blood, Satan knows exactly what is happening, and he comes under dominion and authority.

That kind of power comes straight from the covenant Jesus offered us. To keep the covenant, we have to walk in honor whether anyone else sees it or not.

Husbands, Honor Your Wives

Ye wives, be in subjection to your own husbands.... Likewise, ye husbands, dwell with them according to knowledge, giving honour unto the wife, as unto the weaker vessel, and as being heirs together of the grace of life; that your prayers be not hindered (1 Peter 3:1, 7).

The Word says that husbands are to honor

their wives, treating them with care and kindness
and tenderness.

It also says for wives to honor their own husbands by submitting to them. That does not mean to
be under their thumb and to follow their orders. That
is not being submissive. That is being dominated.
Wives are supposed to submit to their husbands'
honoring of them.

First Peter 3:7 says that husbands should dwell
with their wives "according to knowledge." This
knowledge is knowledge of God's Word. Husbands
and wives are to dwell with each other in honor as
God has explained it in His Word, not according to
some religious tradition.

For too long, women have been relegated to second-
class citizenship in the kingdom of God simply because
proud, foolish men have not understood what the
New Testament really teaches about honor. In their
ignorance and arrogance, such men have built dishonorable religious systems that bind up the hand-
maidens of the Lord.

Some of these men are in for a big surprise. The
husband will find himself carrying around his wife's
Bible for her while she preaches the gospel and wins
souls by the millions.

Hopefully, many of us men in the Church will

begin to realize that our wives are just as much God's children as we are. We will start treating them with the honor God prescribes in His Word.

The Bible teaches that wives are to be submissive to their husbands, and that husbands are to treat their wives with honor *as if* they were weaker vessels, treating them with tenderness and love. This does not mean, however, that women *are* weaker vessels. Men and women are each superior to the other in certain ways. God made them that way. Both are made in His image. "God created man in his own image, in the image of God created he him; male and female created he them" (Genesis 1:27).

That means God is both male and female.

Every word in the Hebrew language has either male or female gender—except one! *Jehovah.* Jehovah is the only word that has both male and female gender; so God is as much female as He is male.

When God made Adam, Adam was both male and female. God separated the female part from Adam and deposited it in Eve. Then He brought them back together to honor one another. Where a man is weak, the woman is strong. Where the woman is weak, the man is strong. United, the two of them should have no weaknesses. They should honor and reverence one another as heirs *together* of the grace of life.

Then together husbands and wives are to submit to God by honoring Him.

Honor One Another

Be kindly affectioned one to another... in honour preferring one another (Romans 12:10).

As husbands and wives, we must honor one another in the Lord.

I'm still learning, but I'm reaching to learn much more from God about how to treat my wife. The Bible says I am to treat her with honor, as unto a weaker vessel. She is not weaker. To tell you the truth, I wouldn't want to get in a fistfight with her! But that is not what this book is all about. It is about honor. So to honor her, I understand that I am to treat my wife as if she were as fragile as glass. I am to treat her as I would a fine, priceless treasure—which she is.

We husbands must start treating our wives right and in honor as God commanded. The honor of God, His covenant with us, will change not only our attitude toward our wives, but also their attitude toward us.

When we live in honor, it brings the Father on the scene.

Many husbands have been treating their wives as mere women. Instead, we are to treat them as children of God. The believing husband is to honor his wife as an heir with him of God's grace. The child of God with whom he shares a marriage covenant is not just his wife. She is his covenant sister in the Lord. She is the daughter of Almighty God!

This woman is an heir of God's grace and a joint heir with Jesus Christ. She does not deserve to be mistreated or abused. She does not deserve to be dominated. She does not deserve to be put in bondage. She deserves honor because she belongs to God just as her husband does.

Honor the covenant Almighty God has offered you. Honor it, and He will honor you—with mercy, love, grace, career satisfaction, marital happiness and prosperity.

Riches and Honor

Happy is the man that findeth wisdom, and the man that getteth understanding. For the merchandise of it is better than the merchandise of silver, and the gain thereof than fine gold. She is more precious than rubies: and all the things thou canst desire are not to be compared unto her. Length of days is in her right hand; and in her left hand riches and honour (Proverbs 3:13-16).

This scripture says Wisdom holds life in one hand and riches and honor in the other. Without honor, wealth—or the prospect of wealth—is dangerous.

As we saw in chapter 3, Proverbs 1:32 says prosperity will ruin a fool. Why? Because a fool will not know how to handle prosperity honorably.

When prosperity ruins a fool, he doesn't know it. He will do everything he can to gain wealth—including running right over you. He is a thief. He will steal your time, even your thought life, by telling you a lie if he thinks it will help him. He will steal your honor to get what he wants.

A dishonorable person will always have money problems. No matter how much wealth he accumulates, he will always be in financial trouble.

A dishonorable person is driven by fear. That is the reason he lies. He is afraid. Afraid of what? Afraid of losing what he does have. He is also afraid of never getting what he wants and doesn't have.

Sadly, many "good" Christians, and even the

Church itself, have adopted this same attitude.

Our thinking has been so perverted by the world's ideas of finance that our attitude has become, "If I get anything, I have to keep it. I must not let it get away." Actually, that is the most selfish, self-defeating attitude a Christian or Christian organization can have. It is also the most dishonorable thing we can do because God gave us the power to get wealth in order to establish His covenant on the earth.

Use what you have to establish God's covenant, to spread His Word throughout the world. The Lord will replace that money if you honor Him and follow the dictates of the covenant. If you are dishonorable and hold tight to what you have, you will never have much more than you do now. You will always be either headed into financial trouble or just coming out of financial trouble, and worried about it all the time.

Be honorable before God and do your part. He will honor you. Believe God for your finances and act on your belief.

If you don't want to keep more than a few hundred dollars a month for yourself and your family, that's your decision. I think you are cheating your family; but that's between you, your family and God. Go ahead and believe God for $10,000, keep a few hundred dollars of it, and put the rest into the work of God.

The blessings of the Lord will start overtaking you if you stay in honor with God and keep His covenant.

God appreciates what you do for Him. He will return it to you faster than you can invest it. I know, because He has done it for me. These blessings will overtake and overwhelm you. God will bless you with riches faster than you can get rid of them. When you begin to honor the covenant by supporting the preaching of the gospel, God will honor you richly.

The Lord has promised, "Those who honor Me, I will honor" (1 Samuel 2:30). What is that honor? Can we identify it in Scripture? Yes, we can. He who is faithful (or honorable) over little will be made master over much (Luke 16:10-12; Matthew 25:21).

Riches and honor come with wisdom and understanding. They are a part of the heritage of the saints—those who honor God with their lives and substance.

chapter 7

BE NOT SLOTHFUL IN BUSINESS

Be kindly affectioned one to another with brotherly love; in honour preferring one another; not slothful in business; fervent in spirit; serving the Lord; rejoicing in hope; patient in tribulation; continuing instant in prayer; distributing to the necessity of saints; given to hospitality (Romans 12:10-13).

God wants us, you and me, to do business. He wants us to do business in honor, in the spirit of the covenant He has given us.

In the spirit, we are covenanted together because we are part of the covenant that Jesus has with the Father. We are in Him—in Jesus.

Is Jesus in you? Are you in Him? He is in me, and I am in Him. If you and I are in Him, then we are in Him together. If He is in me and in you, then you are in me and I am in you.

This has some consequences.

One Body, One Honor

For as the body is one, and hath many members, and all the members of that one body, being many, are one body: so also is Christ. For by one Spirit are we all baptized into one body, whether we be Jews or Gentiles, whether we be bond or free; and have been all made to drink into one Spirit. For the body is not one member, but many.... And whether one member suffer, all the members suffer with it; or one member be honoured, all the members rejoice with it. Now ye are the body of Christ, and members in particular (1 Corinthians 12:12-14, 26-27).

The Bible says that all of us together make up the Body of Christ; and if one member of the Body suffers, we all suffer. For me to dishonor you affects not only you, but also me. It affects the whole Body of Christ. If one of us is honored, or honorable, we all share in that honor. Likewise, if one of us dishonors himself, there are negative consequences for all of us.

God has the power to turn over all the world's finances to us. Until now we have not been worthy of that kind of trust. We would have used that wealth on ourselves. We would have squandered it and used it foolishly, until the devil got hold of it all again.

If all the wealth in the world were divided evenly, every man, woman and child on the face of the earth would receive several million dollars. The figure goes up each day as more assets are discovered. If those assets were evenly distributed today to every individual in the world, in a year's time or so the ones who control it now would have it all back. Unfortunately, that's also true of the Body of Christ and it shouldn't be that way. God's blessings are for every person in Christ Jesus, not just a few.

We are one Body in Christ and each one is a member of the others.

God has given us definite instructions: "Be kindly affectioned one to another with brotherly love; in honour preferring one another...distributing to the necessity of saints..." (Romans 12:10, 13). We are to honor one another—and the Lord—with our material blessings.

God has given you the same thing He has given me. I have to respect the fact that you have eternal life, which only God can give. He bestowed it upon you just as He bestowed it upon me. I have to respect you, because I respect God. The Bible says that if we love the Father who begat, we love him also who is begotten of Him (1 John 5:1).

I don't love you because you are lovable, or because you are not lovable. I love you because you are born of God. God has honored you with His life, His Name and His Spirit. How can I do any less? It really makes no difference how I see your conduct— whether I *think* it is right or wrong. I am to deal with *my* conduct, which is regulated by the covenant I have with Almighty God.

God is the only One who has the right to judge. You and I do not. It does not matter if we think the other person is right or wrong. It's none of our business. Whose business is it? God's.

I asked the Lord one time, "What is the biggest problem in the Body of Christ?" I didn't expect to hear what I heard. He answered me quickly, without hesitation: *Your dogged determination to correct one another.* It's the biggest problem in the Body of Christ. It stops more healings, more faith, more power, more of everything. Our dogged determination to correct people that we have no authority over is dishonorable.

Be Honorable, Not Slothful

Be kindly affectioned one to another with brotherly love; in honour preferring one another; not
slothful in business...(Romans 12:10-11).

The Apostle Paul tells us not to be lazy. There
should not be an unwilling attitude where business
is concerned between Christians. We should not be
lazy and dishonorable in our dealings with anyone,
especially not with our brothers and sisters in Christ.

This almost happened to me. I'm embarrassed to
think how close I came to doing the very thing I am
warning you about.

I remember the day a young fellow came into my
office and said he wanted to see me. I knew his folks
so I let him in. He was excited.

"Brother Copeland," he said, "I've been listening to your tapes, and I've quit my job. I'm living by
faith. I'm going in the ministry full time."

I thought, *Lord, he's going to be back through here
before long begging for money.*

The Lord said, *Well, when he does, give him some.*

What did You say? I answered.

When he does, give him some, repeated the Lord.

Don't ever sit in judgment against another person's faith. You had better pray and believe God for yourself. If you don't think he has the faith to carry this, get in with him and add your faith to his.

The message I received was: *Don't damn another person's faith.*

The young fellow I talked with that day was Jerry Savelle.

I didn't know what I was talking about. But by acting in honor (along with following some pointed guidance from the Lord) I was blessed to have a part in his eventual success and mighty ministry.

The minute Jerry walked out of the room, I realized that God was commissioning me to help teach and train that young man.

I would have missed that whole blessing if I had followed my own instincts and tried to talk him out of what he believed he was called to do.

I came close to being slothful in business (that is, in my business of being sensitive to God and helping spread His Word, directly or indirectly). God directed me to be fervent in spirit, not to doubt when dealing with a Christian brother or when serving the Lord.

Be Fervent in Spirit

...fervent in spirit; serving the Lord; rejoicing in hope; patient in tribulation; continuing instant in prayer; distributing to the necessity of saints; given to hospitality. Bless them which persecute you: bless, and curse not (Romans 12:11-14).

Never lag in zeal or in earnest endeavor. Be aglow and burning with the Spirit, always eagerly and faithfully serving the Lord.

Don't go around with the corners of your mouth hanging down. Put on Jesus. Be like Jesus. Do as He would do.

Rejoice and exalt in hope, says the Apostle Paul. Be steadfast and patient in suffering and tribulation. Be constant in prayer.

In this passage Paul is describing the way we are to act in the Body of Christ. We are to keep our mouths shut about our own trials and tribulations, about our own hurts. We are not to go around rehearsing our problems all the time, repeating them to every preacher, minister and counselor we run across—again and again.

One of the reasons that we ministers of the gospel sometimes have to avoid our fellow Christians at meetings is because we cannot stay under the anointing if we constantly and repeatedly are being burdened with other people's trials and tribulations. Many people who do this don't really want help. They just want to go over their problems again and again and again, drawing attention to themselves. That's dishonorable.

God has said that our hurts are very important to Him (1 Peter 5:7). However, they ought to mean little or nothing to us. We should be paying very little attention to our own problems and difficulties other than to take our stand of faith on God's Word and roll our cares over on Him and leave them there. He wants us to be alive with hope, not going around saying that things are hopeless all the time.

Be alive with hope. Be steadfast and patient in suffering. Don't worry about what is coming against you. Be strong in faith. Belittle your problems in the presence of others.

Quit carrying your burdens and cares around everywhere you go. Distribute to the needs of God's people. Share in meeting the necessities of the saints. Pursue the practice of hospitality. Bless those who persecute you, those who are cruel in their attitude toward you. Bless, and do not curse.

Be About the Business

I must be about my Father's business
(Luke 2:49).

God does not want us to be slothful in conducting our business. He has honored us by giving it to
us. We have to honor our obligation to Him by running that business or doing that job to the best of our
abilities to do it in faith.

I'll give you an example. God has given me this
ministry. He has given me the calling to minister. I
have to honor that call and duty. I made a decision
that I am going to live responsibly and honorably. I
know Jesus wants me to do that, so I am determined
to do it.

I promised God that any time I was called on
to preach or minister, I would be ready; I would be
prepared. That does not mean I want to all the time.
It does not mean I am constantly, consistently prayed
up and ready to go just on a second's notice. Most of
the time I know in advance when I am going to preach.
I promised the Lord that I would never take time
for myself and my own wants during the periods I
should be preparing to minister to other people.

I am responsible for a prophetic ministry. When I travel from place to place on behalf of the Lord, I don't sightsee. I have been all over the world and have hardly seen anything but airports, hotels and convention centers. I don't go for pleasure or relaxation. I don't go to visit or fellowship. I go to do business. I take seriously Jesus' instructions to His disciples as He sent them out to minister. He said, "When you find a worthy house, stay there" (Matthew 10:11, author's paraphrase). I don't run all over town. I come prepared, ready to settle down and attend to business—my Father's business.

I learned this originally from Oral Roberts; then I found it in the Word of God. Later, I saw it in Kenneth E. Hagin and in other anointed men of God.

I have certain time limits that I just won't violate. I may be in your presence sometime, look at my watch and say, "Excuse me, it's time to go." I do that because I am determined to have God's anointing on me. It is only with the anointing that I can, in turn, be of help to you at all. It is only through the anointing that I can minister effectively to others.

That is the reason all of my children are in the ministry. That is the reason there is romance in our family: between Gloria and me, our children and their mates

and our grandchildren. My family and I honor the
business—the ministry—that God has given us. We
honor one another, uplifting one another at all times.
As a result we enjoy the blessing of God upon us.

Honor Makes a Difference

I will be the first to admit that I was not always
this devoted and committed.

Back in the late '50s I was running from the
Church. I planned never to attend one again. Then,
just to please my father, I attended a meeting of the
Full Gospel Businessmen's Fellowship. What a joy
it was to hear testimonies of men who affirmed that
God was in their businesses. Before that time, we
never heard such men stand up and talk about God.
If they prayed, they were hiding in their prayer closet
somewhere so no one would know about it. None of
them ever wanted to say anything about God out in
the open.

This event was like a breath of fresh, clean air. It
caught my attention. A group of Christian businessmen
got my attention that night. My dad was part of
the chapter in Fort Worth, Texas. One of the first
men I heard speak was Lester Sumrall. The minute
I heard him I knew I was in the presence of a real

man—a man of God.

When I walked into that room, those men started hugging me. I had never seen anything like it! I was being treated like I was somebody. That got my attention. The Full Gospel Businessmen's Fellowship had gotten the attention of businessmen all over the world who woke up to the importance of honor and integrity in business and dealing with others because of the organization's influence in their own lives.

At this point in my life I had spent a lot of time in the entertainment business. I would much rather have been John Wayne than Kenneth Copeland. I also liked to lie. When someone asked me a question, I would lie just to see if I could get them to believe it. I said ugly things, too, just to see people cringe. It was terrible.

My wife said to me one time: "I'm never going out in public with you again as long as I live. You've got the nastiest mouth I've ever heard." And she was right.

I was foulmouthed, and I lied habitually. It was a game I played. I knew it was wrong, but there was a spirit dogging me. Then I came to the Lord.

The very first thing God did was clean up my speech. He took the profanity and the lying out of my mouth the night I got saved. That was a night I will never forget.

The devil tried to tell me, *Oh man, you're just on*

some kind of emotional kick.

I was—and I'm still on one! I knew my experience with the Lord was real because something had changed within me. There was peace on the inside of me, and I had no desire to lie or curse.

What was working in me? God's honor.

All of a sudden I had a desire to be honorable. I didn't want to lie or be foulmouthed. Today, I have a new desire—a new spirit within me.

As you develop the honor of God in your life, it begins to work in your heart, in your marriage, in your business, in your career. The hard decisions are already made once you decide to live and walk by faith—a life walk. You do your part, God does His part. The devil does his part and runs!

Honor Is Important in Business

There is a man I want to tell you about. His story will help you see just how important it is to have honor in business—important in ways you may not have imagined.

This fellow was about 20 years old and had a good job. He came from a family that had very little money. He was the youngest child, and there was a lot of difficulty in his household. He worked his regular job all day, and at night fixed cars to sell. Gradually, he began making money.

He finally saved enough so he could buy a better type of car to restore and sell. He began to make a bit more money. He was good at his work, a gifted businessman.

His folks attended a Baptist church in Fort Worth. There was a meeting at church, and he decided to go. At the end of the service when the invitation was given, the conviction of the Holy Ghost came on him as he stood there. He had a tight grip on the seat in front of him, trying to resist responding to the wooing of the Lord.

The Spirit of God was all over him, and he was trying to keep from going forward and re-ceiving Jesus as his Savior and Lord. A man in the church came over, put his arm around the young man and told him he loved him. He encouraged him to go forward. In fact, that man walked with him down the aisle.

Before that week was up, the same man who had led him to the altar to accept Jesus beat him out of all of his profit on a car. It wasn't a mis-take. He just skinned that young man in a deal—on purpose. The older man should have known better. Any Christian ought to know that you don't get a man saved on Saturday night, then cheat him on Tuesday. That's wrong.

The young man had a temper. He was angry, so he rebelled against the Lord. He said he never would go back to church again. And he didn't.

He became very successful in the car business, and eventually had a business that was nationwide. Then he went into the airplane business, and I started flying for him. He and I became close friends.

My mother and father lived just two doors down from him. He liked my parents and would sometimes eat with us. Mama would feed him and preach to him and just love him. She would say, "I'm telling you right now, I'm going to pray you into the kingdom of God." He would just smile.

She prayed for him just as she prayed for me— all the time. She treated him as if he were her own son, and he just ate it up. But she could not get him inside the church door. Why? Because of a dishonorable Christian businessman.

Years later, after I had entered the ministry I had the opportunity to pray with him. He stayed with it for a few days, then went right back to the way he had been. Afterward, he stayed on my mind and heart a lot. I was praying about his situation once while I was in a meeting and I thought to myself, *I'm going to call him as soon as I get back to town.*

When I got home and called him, a lady answered. When I asked if I could speak to him, she said, "He died day before yesterday."

You can imagine how I felt. I thought, *I missed him.* Although I rolled the grief and pain over on the Lord, something in my spirit would not let it end that way.

I went to the funeral, and the man's son asked me to say a few words about his father. So I did. I told the people exactly what had happened in this man's life, what had caused him to be the way he was.

After the funeral when we were gathered at the memorial park, a woman walked up to me and said, "Kenneth, I need to tell you something." I want you to see God's faithfulness and honor from what she told me.

God's Honor Came Through

I didn't know this woman. I had seen her, but was not acquainted with her personally.

"A few nights ago I absolutely could not sleep," she told me. "I tossed and turned, and finally got up to pray. 'God, what is this?' I asked.

"Get dressed, He answered. *I've got somewhere I want you to go.*

"It was the middle of the night. I usually don't do

things like that, but I obeyed the Lord. I got dressed, and then I asked, 'Where am I supposed to go?'

"He led me to the hospital, so I went.

"'I don't know anybody in this hospital,' I said. 'What do I do now, Lord?'

"He didn't say anything, so I just started praying in the spirit as I walked down each hall. I don't know how many corridors I walked down, but it was several. I went along quietly just praying in the spirit, listening for the Lord. Suddenly I stopped right in front of one room. The Lord said, *Go in there.*

"I went in and saw that the man in the bed wasn't asleep. I walked up to him and said, 'Sir, I don't know you, and you don't know me. But the Lord wouldn't let me sleep tonight. God sent me down here to you. Do you know Jesus as Lord?'

"He said, 'You sound like Vinita and Kenneth Copeland.'

"'Vinita Copeland is a close personal friend of mine,' I told him.

"'I've been trying to call Kenneth for two days,' he answered. "He's out of town, and I was lying here praying, 'God give me somebody. I'm dying. Send me somebody. I can't die in this shape. I can't die like this. Send me somebody, Lord. Send me somebody.'"

What was happening in that situation? God's

honor was at work. God was honoring the decision that man made back in the Baptist church nearly 40 years before. He was honoring my mother's prayers and my prayers and our love for that man. God was honoring all these things.

Thank God for that woman who honored God's direction to go to that hospital in the middle of the night, not even knowing why. She prayed with him, and he came back to Jesus, praying and rejoicing in Him.

Then he died.

Actually, he didn't die. He just stepped out of that old cancerous body in which he was confined and went on to be with the Lord.

Think what just one act by a dishonorable Christian had done. Because of that one shameful dealing, another man had spent his entire life out of fellowship with Jesus, his brothers and sisters in the Lord, and with the Father Himself. But this man finally recognized the honor of God in the last minute of the last hour. Thank God for that!

Prefer One Another in Honor

Let every soul be subject unto the higher powers. For there is no power but of God: the powers that be are ordained of God.

Whosoever therefore resisteth the power, resisteth the ordinance of God: and they that
resist shall receive to themselves damnation
[condemnation] (Romans 13:1-2).

Paul says that anyone who resists civil authority
resists the authority of God and will receive damnation
or condemnation. This is a continuation of Romans
12 in which Paul was speaking about the Christian
Church, the Body of Christ, acting and preferring one
another in honor. He warns that if we do not honor
one another, including those in authority over us, the
devil will move in our households and destroy us.

What if the government is totally against
Christianity and threatens to imprison anyone for
preaching the gospel? That is a dishonorable government. No question about it. But that does not
mean the people in office are not ordained of God.
It means they are ignoring the ordination that God
has placed upon them. It is available to them if
they only knew it.

What the Lord is saying here through the
Apostle Paul is that Christians still carry honor
about them, even in the midst of a crooked and
perverse generation.

The people in East Germany got hold of the Word

of God concerning the authority of the believer. They prayed and believed God, asking Him for guidance and deliverance. I have talked to pastors in that totalitarian, anti-Christian society who had to operate underground for years. Every one of them said to me: "We had to learn to love those political leaders who were trying their best to damn us to hell. We walked in honor. We began to see that we could pull down those demonic powers that were opposed to us and to the gospel of Jesus Christ."

Our fight is not against flesh and blood (Ephesians 6:12).

These men said they prayed and asked God for their situation to be changed without bloodshed, and it was.

It was a different story in Romania. The believers there, although lovely Christian people, were not walking in a revelation of their authority from God, so their deliverance has not been as quick or as complete and certainly not without bloodshed.

A Dishonorable People

And even as they did not like to retain God in their knowledge, God gave them over to a reprobate mind, to do those things which are not convenient (Romans 1:28).

There are occasions when those ordained of God to be in government absolutely and totally refuse the Lord. They have no desire for God. They vote Him out. This has happened here in the United States. The Bible says in Romans 1:28 that such people are given over to a reprobate mind, or to a mind of false judgment.

When people vote God out, He leaves. That's simple. He will not stay where He is not wanted. He takes His influence and departs, turning over to a reprobate mind those who refuse Him. He withdraws His blessing as well as His presence. Those who turn Him away end up not being able to balance their checkbook, much less the national budget.

What is wrong with our nation today? A loss of honor.

This dishonor is not only evident in the government but also it is seen in the Church. We Christian people, instead of maintaining our honor, have acted just like the rest of society. We have been treating one another shamefully for a long time, acting as if we don't want God in our knowledge—ignoring His commandments. We raise up committees and vote people out of the church. We have fine, beautiful buildings, but we don't let sinners in—unless they look, dress, talk, act and believe like we do.

We ask, "Why doesn't God help us in our churches anymore?" Because we are a dishonorable people. Though we have honor in us, we are not acting on it. It is the same as having faith and not acting on it.

We have the love of God in us by His Spirit (Romans 5:5), but that does not mean we always exercise it. In the same way, we have God's honor born into us. The problem is that we have not always demonstrated and lived by that honor. Part of living honorably is giving due respect and obedience to God-ordained authority.

It Is Honorable to Be Subject to Authority

For rulers are not a terror to good works, but to the evil. Wilt thou then not be afraid of the power? do that which is good, and thou shalt have praise of the same: for he is the minister of God to thee for good. But if thou do that which is evil, be afraid; for he beareth not the sword in vain: for he is the minister of God, a revenger to execute wrath upon him that doeth evil. Wherefore ye must needs be subject, not only for wrath, but also for conscience sake (Romans 13:3-5).

Here is one place where most Christians have not

acted in honor. They have quit praying for the police officer, who is a minister of God. He is often treated like a dog—the way the drug crowd treats him—as though he doesn't belong. He and the dangerous life he faces are often ignored, as though he were a second-class citizen or less.

However, in Little Rock, Ark., Pastor Happy Caldwell and his church are changing all this. They divide up the names of all the officers in the police department and the sheriff's office—all the civil authority in that city. The names are handed out to people in the church who take those law-enforcement agents before God in prayer. The believers intercede and make supplication in the spirit for the law officers in that area. The names are rotated, so there is a different person praying for each one of them on a regular schedule.

These prayer warriors have had a grand influence on that city and its crime level.

Godly Prayer Is Honorable

I exhort therefore, that, first of all, supplications, prayers, intercessions, and giving of thanks, be made for all men; for kings, and for all that are in authority; that we may lead a quiet and peaceable life in all godliness and honesty (1 Timothy 2:1-2).

According to this scripture, we are to pray not only for those in authority, but also for all men.

Sometimes when I see on television that someone has committed a violent crime, I pray about that situation.

I say, "Father, I pray in the Name of Jesus. First of all, I ask that You protect the officers who are involved in this investigation. Second, I ask that You send Your ministering angels to reveal to those officers where to find the suspect they're seeking."

I have two reasons for praying this way, besides asking for the protection of those who serve the Lord as His ministers of justice. First, the person who committed that crime needs to be caught and taken off the streets. Second, if he is apprehended there is a chance to get him saved. There is more revival going on today in penitentiaries than in some churches.

As Christians we are to prefer one another. We are to honor those in positions of rightful authority over us. We are to give them due respect and obedience, and remember to pray for them consciously, consistently and continually—even those who oppose and oppress us. That is the honorable thing to do.

chapter 8

HONOR BETWEEN GOD AND MAN

Therefore if any man be in Christ, he is a new creature: old things are passed away; behold, all things are become new. And all things are of God, who hath reconciled us to himself by Jesus Christ, and hath given to us the ministry of reconciliation; to wit [to know], that God was in Christ, reconciling the world unto himself, not imputing their trespasses unto them; and hath committed unto us the word of reconciliation. Now then we are ambassadors for Christ, as though God did beseech you by us: we pray you in Christ's stead, be ye reconciled to God (2 Corinthians 5:17-20).

It's time to examine a little more closely the relationship of honor between man and God. In previous chapters, we have looked at bits and pieces.

Let's put it all together.

You remember we talked about the fact that to

honor is to delegate authority. That works both ways. When you and I humble ourselves before God, we delegate to Him authority over our lives. It has rarely been preached this way, but I believe it should have been. In the future this is how we should think of honor.

We have been backward about some of these things over the years. We need to tell people when they come to Jesus, "You are a unique human being. There never has been anyone exactly like you, and there never will be. As far as God is concerned, you are unique, one of a kind. You can never be replaced. You are not expendable."

It doesn't matter what kind of life you have lived or how deep in the jaws of hell you may be. Jesus has already died for you. As far as God is concerned your fate has already been decided. The Bible says that God reconciled us to Himself through the blood of Jesus Christ, His Son. Now it is up to us to reconcile ourselves to Him, because He has already reconciled Himself to us.

God is not willing to do without any person. We need to tell people that it is an honor to God, an honor to Jesus, for someone to come to Him and say: "Lord, I turn my life over to You. I give You my spirit, my soul and my body. Everything I am and everything I have, I submit to You. You are my Lord and my God. Take complete power and authority and dominion over me." You are the only person who has the authority to give yourself. Only you can make that decision.

It is an honor to God for us to do that. He has promised that when we honor Him, He will honor us.

Honor Only We Can Bestow

Nobody on the face of this earth has the power and authority to give us to God, but we ourselves. What an honor it is when He accepts us and, in return, bestows upon us all that is His.

When we were saved, we gave Him all that we had. It wasn't much, but it was all we could give. What more important thing could anyone give to God than himself? Ourselves plus our time is all we have to give. Once we do that, then everything else we give to Him becomes an honor. Even though the tithe is His from the start, when we bring to God what is His, He counts it as an honor. Why? Because He is honorable.

God Is Honorable

When the Lord says, "Do unto others as you would have them do unto you," He is not saying that just so He can boss us around. He is saying it to enhance the quality of our lives. He knows that if we practice the Golden Rule, doing unto others as we would have them do unto us, eventually we will be surrounded by people who are doing the same thing to us. That's a spiritual law. Whatsoever a person sows that shall he also reap.

A sword has two edges on it. There is an uncanny system of balance in God's plan. It doesn't matter how long or how hard anyone may fight it, it can't be stopped. Watch it over the years. It may not happen instantaneously, but it will happen. The hundredfold return has a front side and a back side. All Scripture does. Every scripture that will bless also will curse.

The Word of God says we will have what we say. It does not say we will have only what we say that is good. It just says we will have whatever we say. Now, this comes to play very seriously in the study of living honorably before God and man. When you and I act in honor, or honorably, even if we have to swear to our own hurt, we bring our heavenly Father on the scene.

God says that whoever honors Him will be honored by Him (1 Samuel 2:30). Honor is a powerful spiritual force. It is an act of the will, an act which triggers covenant realities.

Our will is what governs our life, not our spirit. I like to illustrate it the way God illustrated it to me when I was a young boy.

Honor and the Will

When I was a boy, my dad was quite a fisherman. Often he would take me along, and I loved it.

Dad traveled for a living, and I missed him while he was gone. The day he was due home, I could hardly wait. Sometimes when he came in, he would say we were getting up early the next day to go fishing.

The evening before our trip I couldn't sleep. I would get up in the middle of the night, make sure my tackle box was full, and lay out my fishing clothes. Then I would wake up at 4 o'clock the next morning. When Dad came in to get me up, I would already be dressed, with rod, reel and tackle box in my hands. I was ready because we were going fishing. It was glorious!

Now the same man could come home from his travels, tell me something different and get a totally opposite reaction from me. He could say we were going to get up early the next morning to work in the yard. Strangely, I wouldn't be eager at all. Why not? Because yardwork was my idea of absolutely nothing to do. Even today, I feel about it like President George H.W. Bush does about broccoli—I don't like it. Never have. If it were left up to me, we would cement the whole yard, paint it green and forget it.

Gloria can go out there and dig and scratch around in that dirt all she wants to. I will buy her all the tools she wants. But as long as I have a choice, I'll leave all that yardwork up to her and whoever else she can find to help her.

As for mowing grass, there isn't a lawn mower made that is fine enough to make me want to use it. I have no desire to work in the yard, whatever the enticement. If someone ever invents one that will fly, I might like to try it a time or two just to see what it's like. Other than that, I'm not interested.

When I knew we were going to get up early to work in the yard, my response was not the same as when we were going fishing. I didn't wake up during the night and look for my working clothes. The next morning when Dad came to wake me, I wasn't up and ready, smiling with a hoe in my hand—I was sound asleep. He had to call me at least three times. Even then I had to drag myself out of bed.

What was the difference? My will. My dad was the same man in both instances. I loved him just as much in either case. Whether we were going fishing or digging, I felt exactly the same about him. I willed to go fishing. I didn't will to do yardwork.

Our will determines whether we act with enthusiasm or with dread, in faith or in fear, and whether we act on what God says or on what the devil says. It is like a thermostat on the wall. The thermostat has no power to cool a room. It just sends a signal to the air conditioner telling it that "the room temperature has reached the point that some cool air is needed." This alerts the air conditioner to turn on until the thermostat says, "OK, that's enough."

Like that thermostat, our will sends out information—requests and commands. Do you need healing? Your faith won't come in line until the thermostat of your will sends a message: "Healing, please."

It makes no difference what sickness it is, whether cancer or a head cold. Your body doesn't know the difference, and your will and faith shouldn't either. There is no law, no demon, that can overcome faith. Only you personally control your faith.

On a hot day, if you set the thermostat on HEAT rather than COOL, don't expect pleasing results. Don't make that same mistake with your will and your faith. Don't say, "Fear, please," and expect to get faith's results.

We have done the Lord a terrible injustice by not

honoring Him, by not receiving from Him what He wants to do for us, through us and about us. Why have we done Him this injustice? Because of our lack of knowledge, our lack of will.

We did the same thing for a long time with the Holy Spirit: refused to receive Him. We did the same thing then with the gifts of the Spirit: refused to receive them.

What happens when we use our will to honor God? The Father honors us in return. He says to us: "Because you have honored Me, I will honor you. You are acting in honor, so the honorable thing for Me to do is to take care of you. You are obedient to Me, so I will be obedient to you." You draw nigh to God and He will draw nigh to you (James 4:8).

The Lord asked me one time, *Kenneth, will you do anything I ask you to do?*

"Yes, Lord," I answered. "You know I will."

I know you will, He responded. *But you don't understand that I will do anything you ask Me to do.*

I could hardly believe my ears.

"What did You say, Lord?"

I said that I will do anything you ask Me to do.

Jesus says this in John 16:23: "Whatsoever ye shall ask the Father in my name, he will give it you."

I didn't believe that, though. I believed I would

do anything God asked me to do, but I wasn't really sure He would do anything for me.

There I was—born again, a man of faith and prayer, who was out preaching the gospel—but I had no idea God would do whatever I asked in Jesus' Name. I did pray correctly, and I did have prayers answered, but that kind of thought had never entered my mind.

Kenneth, don't you realize that I am far more committed to you than you are to Me? asked the Lord. *I loved you before you were ever saved. I loved you even before you were born again. I gave My life for you.*

That stirred me to the soles of my feet.

Honoring God With Praise

Praise ye the Lord. Sing unto the Lord a new song, and his praise in the congregation of saints. Let Israel rejoice in him that made him: let the children of Zion be joyful in their King. Let them praise his name in the dance: let them sing praises unto him with the timbrel and harp. For the Lord taketh pleasure in his people: he will beautify the meek with salvation. Let the saints be joyful in glory: let them sing aloud upon their beds. Let the high praises of God be in their mouth, and a twoedged sword in their hand; to execute vengeance upon the heathen, and punishments upon the people; to bind their kings with chains, and their nobles with fetters of iron; to execute upon them the judgment written: this honour have all his saints. Praise ye the Lord (Psalm 149).

What is the sword in our hand that has two edges? The Word of God. It is sharper than any two-edged sword. Its purpose is to execute vengeance upon the heathen.

In the New Testament, this two-edged sword is part of the full armor of God we use in our spiritual warfare (Ephesians 6:11-17). We must remember, however, that "we wrestle not against flesh and blood, but against principalities, against powers, against the rulers of the darkness of this world, against spiritual wickedness in high places" (verse 12).

We are to use the sword of the Spirit to execute vengeance upon the forces of darkness and punishment upon Satan, to bind the rulers of darkness with chains and their nobles with fetters of iron, to execute against them the written judgment. This honor belongs to all the saints of God. (See Psalm 149:7-9.) The Church of Jesus Christ has been given the honor of using Jesus' Name to cast out the devil.

The Bible says that glory and honor are in the Lord's presence (1 Chronicles 16:27). When we speak in the Name of Jesus, the devil has to do what we say, because God Almighty is in us and works through us. When we stand firm with that two-edged sword held in our hand and coming out our mouth, we are in the presence of God, which gives us glory and honor.

Crowned With Glory and Honor

But one in a certain place testified, saying, What is man, that thou art mindful of him? or the son of man, that thou visitest him? Thou madest him a little lower than the angels; thou crownedst him with glory and honour, and didst set him over the works of thy hands: Thou hast put all things in subjection under his feet. For in that he put all in subjection under him, he left nothing that is not put under him. But now we see not yet all things put under him. But we see Jesus, who was made a little lower than the angels for the suffering of death, crowned with glory and honour (Hebrews 2:6-9).

As we have already seen in Psalm 8, God created man and crowned him with honor and glory (verse 5). Then it tells us what that honor was. That honor was dominion over all the works of His hands (verse 6). Adam's act of dishonor gave that dominion to Satan; but he lost more than just dominion over the works of God's hands. He lost the life of God that was in his spirit.

God said, "The day you eat that fruit, you will surely die." Well, Adam's physical body didn't fall dead. His spirit lost its life that day. It was separated from God. His body lived 930 years longer.

In Hebrews 2 we read that Jesus was crowned with glory and honor. All things have been put under subjection to Him. That includes life itself. He regained what Adam lost.

Authority of the Believer

No man in *himself* has authority over God or what belongs to Him. God has authority over it, and He has given that authority both in heaven and earth to Jesus.

It makes some religious folks mad when we talk about the authority of the believer. I've never been able to figure out why. It makes no sense to me. God's people should be hungry to learn about their

God-given rights and responsibilities.

By now it ought to have become clear to us that God is not going to do everything in life for us. Why? Because most things are in our realm of authority and responsibility.

Suppose somebody were to break into your garage and steal your lawn mower. When you call the police, one of the first questions you would be asked is, "Was the garage locked?" You wouldn't say, "No, I've got faith in the police." They are faithful and devoted to duty; but if you are not willing to lock your garage, how can they help you?

That is the way religious people have been about the works of Satan.

One of the very first things Jesus did after being raised from the dead was to honor the Church by crowning it with glory and honor. In Matthew 28, He said that all power and all authority had been given unto Him, both in heaven and in earth. He ordered His followers to go into all the earth and operate in His Name. What higher authority is there? His Name is above every name that is named, in heaven, in earth and under the earth (Ephesians 1:21; Philippians 2:9-10).

Then He gave us His full armor. He told us to receive the Holy Spirit and become His witnesses in all the earth (Acts 1:8). We are to do what He does, say what He says and act like He acts. He has promised that He will be with us even to the end of the world (Matthew 28:20).

The devil will flee before us. But not if we don't exercise the God-given power, authority and dominion that is ours as sons and daughters of the Most High God. Not if we don't have the will to trigger the faith that allows us to use the spiritual weapons that God has given us.

Our authority is not based on our strength or power. It is based on the Word of God. Let the Word fight its own battles. God has honored us with the authority to use His Word, knowing that as we do so He will honor it.

God Honors His Word

Let me share two stories that illustrate just how honorable the Lord is when it comes to His Word.

The first story has to do with the faith of a family. A young man, who was a tennis pro, had a cancer. In a very short period of time, it grew from the size of a golf ball until it was nine inches in diameter.

The doctors had given him only 10 hours to live—10 hours to get healed. That is not the time

to decide to become a student of the Bible. The best
time to become a student of the Word of God is long
before the onset of such a dire situation.

This young man's family laid hold on the Word
of God and would not let go. They began claiming
God's promise of healing—and they didn't stop.
While in his room, there was someone either
reading Scripture or praying every minute of every
hour. Instead of 10 hours, he lived for several days,
then several weeks, then several months. Today he
is back on the tennis circuit.

The important thing is that his family refused
to let go, not for even a minute. They looked to the
Lord 24 hours a day. I have seen that happen before.

A friend of ours had a son who fell to the bottom of a huge empty grain elevator. There was a
Holy Spirit-baptized police officer just a block or two
away, and the Spirit of God spoke to him. He whirled
his squad car around and headed full speed in the
opposite direction.

His partner asked, "What are you doing?"

"I don't know."

He drove to that grain elevator, jumped out of the
car, found that young man and had him in the hospital in a matter of minutes.

The boy's mother came to the hospital and

stationed herself there. She stood over her son with the boldness of a lion, telling everyone in sight, "You aren't coming in here with unbelief."

She put the Word of God on tape and played it in her son's ear night and day. If the nurses didn't like it, she ran them out. If the doctors objected, she made them leave. Their opinions made no difference to her. She honored God's Word above the opinions of men.

All the time that she had a tape player plugged into her son's ear, the doctors were saying he would never regain consciousness. Then he started coming around. They told her, "Even if he survives, he'll always be a vegetable." But he wasn't a vegetable. They claimed, "He'll never walk." Then he started walking.

One doctor got so mad early in the process that he finally said to her: "You're the biggest fool I've ever seen. When that boy dies, it's going to destroy your hope and faith."

"We'll see," she told him. She stood her ground.

When people came in and started to give her their condolences, she would say, "Either talk faith in here, or don't talk at all." Since they knew the boy was in a coma, they thought he couldn't hear; but he could. His spirit understood everything that was said in that room. His flesh was injured, not his spirit.

Most of the well-meaning, Bible-toting Christians gave up on that boy. They just "knew" he was going to die. Why? Because of a lack of diligence, a lack of stirring, a lack of feeding of the inner man on a daily basis.

Many Christians lose their faith when they are in the presence of unbelievers, especially in emergency situations. Why? Because the believers' faith is weak. Their faith had no strength in it and no substance to it long before the people of unbelief came along. Thank God, the families in the two situations I described had real faith, not imitation faith.

Run from the deathsayers. They are not of God. God honors His Word. If you honor God, He will honor you and His promises to you. Stay stirred up—be alive in the Spirit. Keep your ear open to God and His Word.

Protect your spirit. It contains both your will and your faith. Out of it flow the forces of life (Proverbs 4:23). Faith is in there. Your will is in there. The righteousness of God is in there. The love of God is in there. The joy of the Lord is in there. All of the fruit of the spirit is in there: love, joy, peace, longsuffering, gentleness, goodness, faith, meekness and temperance (Galatians 5:22-23).

Know Your Needs

But my God shall supply all your need according to his riches in glory by Christ Jesus (Philippians 4:19).

Know exactly what your needs are. Quit guessing about them. You are promised that God will meet your needs. Take time to find out what your needs are.

I used to think my needs were just food on my table, clothes on my back and a roof over my head. After I began to pray about it, I came to realize that I was cheating myself and other people because I was limiting my needs.

As I continued to pray and seek God, I discovered that my needs included much more than my own basic necessities. They included my church, my pastor and other ministries. They included going out into all the world and preaching the gospel to every creature. That is an assignment of every Christian.

Possess the Land

Every place that the sole of your foot shall tread

upon, that have I given unto you, as I said unto Moses (Joshua 1:3).

You and I may not be able to go to all the world, but we can go to our own neighborhood. Most of us would rather go around the world than right next door.

Like I said earlier, I don't like to mow yards, not even my own, but one day the Lord told me to mow my neighbor's yard.

"Lord," I asked, "You want me to mow that man's yard? The grass is about six inches high. What if he's home? If he looks outside and sees me out there mowing his yard, he may get upset."

Then I happened to think: *If I saw somebody out mowing my yard, I wouldn't complain. I might be embarrassed, but I would be grateful. I wouldn't say a word to him—until he got through!*

Still my mind kept trying to talk me out of what God had told me to do.

Do it the way Joshua did, the Lord said. *He claimed every part of the ground where his foot stepped. Go over there, mow that man's yard and claim that family for the kingdom.*

So I did.

Later I found out that my neighbor was out of town. That's why his grass was so tall.

Sometime before, I had met the man and his wife. They had two boys that played with our son John. One afternoon while the boys were playing, one of them happened to get his finger mashed in the swing. He screamed so loudly you could have heard him all over the neighborhood. John came running in saying, "Daddy, come pray! Come pray quick!" I ran out, grabbed that little fellow's finger and said, "In the Name of Jesus, I command the pain in this finger to stop. Be healed, in Jesus' Name."

His eyes were like saucers, and his mouth dropped open. After a moment he said, "That's the dumbest thing I ever heard in my life."

I got so tickled that I laughed out loud.

"How's your finger?" I asked.

"Oh, I've got to go home," he responded without answering my question. His finger was healed instantly, and he hadn't even thought about it, because I had shocked him so badly by doing "the dumbest thing he had ever heard in his life."

Well, a few days later there came a knock on my front door. I opened it, and I have never been witnessed to so fast and so hard in my life. The lady said, "Mr. Copeland, did you know that Jesus Christ of Nazareth is alive today? He was raised from the dead!"

It was the boy's mother from next door, just

preaching away. She was not very tall, but by the time she got through with me, she looked like she was six feet four inches! She just kept shouting and witnessing to me about the Lord. Finally, she began to wind down. She was going to close the deal and get me saved.

"Listen," I said. "Hold on a minute."

She backed up for a second, and I quickly explained: "Let me tell you something. I'm a born-again child of the living God, and I'm a preacher. That's what I do. I believe every word you said."

"Glory be to God!" she exclaimed.

"What in the world happened to you?" I asked. "This hasn't been on you very long."

"No, just a few days. There was a lay witness mission in a church right down the street there." She was talking so fast she could hardly get the words out of her mouth. "My husband and I went and discovered that Jesus loves us. I'm going to start a children's prayer group right here in the neighborhood. Can your children come?"

"Yes, they surely can," I said.

What had happened? All I did was mow that yard, but I did it in faith. I did it glorifying God, and God did what He had been wanting to do through me. He needed my faith and my obedience. All I did was provide God the open door that He wanted.

Know exactly what your needs are. I had to learn to include my neighbors in my needs. Don't short-change yourself or those around you—your family, your neighbors, your church, your world. God is not going to rebuke you for needing too much.

Humility Precedes Blessing

Be of the same mind one toward another. Mind not high things, but condescend to men of low estate. Be not wise in your own conceits (Romans 12:16).

Did you ever read in the Bible where Jesus cursed a fig tree because it had so many figs on it that some of them fell off and rotted? No, of course you didn't. It doesn't say that. He cursed the one that would not produce (Matthew 21:19).

God expects us to be fruitful, to produce enough to meet our own needs and the needs of many others. This is good stewardship of God's resources.

We must come before God in prayer, being honest with ourselves and with Him about our needs. It takes time with the Lord to know what the key issues and real needs are. Many times it's important to know the difference between needs and wants.

Our wants are also very important to God. Our heavenly Father is not against our wanting. What He is opposed to is our seeking after things to promote and exalt ourselves. There is nothing wrong with our being exalted—if we are exalted by God and not by ourselves. The Bible says, "Humble yourselves therefore under the mighty hand of God, that he may exalt you in due time" (1 Peter 5:6).

God does not mind our being exalted over the devil and over his demons. Jesus did that for us. It is when we exalt ourselves over other people that we get into trouble. According to Romans 12:10, we are to prefer one another in honor. Then in verse 16 we are told not to become conceited. If we are running after money, property or anything else that will make us bigger in our own eyes and in the eyes of other people, it is wrong.

There is not a thing wrong with wanting to have enough money not only to meet our own needs, but also to finance the work of the Lord. That is rightly stewarding God's resources.

Prospering God's Way

The Lord is my shepherd; I shall not want....

Thou preparest a table before me in the presence of mine enemies: thou anointest my head
with oil; my cup runneth over (Psalm 23:1, 5).

If you want to be prosperous, if you want to
have your needs met, start doing what the Word tells
you to do. Start giving instead of wishing. Start
the giving process, even if you have to start small.
That's all right. Just remember, you are giving into
a much larger Body—the Body of Christ.

Too many Christians are not claiming much of
God's bounty. They are just claiming the crumbs. I
want more than just the crumbs from the mighty
table of God. I'm going to pull up to the table and
have my fill. You need to do that, too.

I was especially blessed by Brother Kenneth Hagin
in a meeting one time. He was speaking from Psalm 23
about the table that has been spread for us by the
Lord in the presence of our enemies. The psalmist
can't be talking about heaven, he pointed out, because there are no enemies in heaven. The table that
has been spread before us is here and now.

Because God is my Shepherd, I do not want.

I don't want for healing. I don't want for
deliverance. I don't want for anything. My Shepherd takes care of all my needs according to His

riches in glory by Christ Jesus.

I don't owe anything to anybody anywhere on the face of this planet, but I didn't get to that place by wishing for it. (We do have monthly expenses, such as television, and they are paid as we are billed.) Gloria and I settled our needs before God. I will tell you frankly what I had to do to settle it, and you can do the same thing.

Take Communion. Lift the cup of the covenant, then lift the bread and say: "Thank You, Jesus. I remember that You cut this covenant for me. I remember that You shed Your blood for me. I remember, Lord."

Jesus, Our Blood Brother

For both he that sanctifieth and they who are sanctified are all of one: for which cause he is not ashamed to call them brethren (Hebrews 2:11).

Let us therefore come boldly unto the throne of grace, that we may obtain mercy, and find grace to help in time of need (Hebrews 4:16).

I don't know why it is so hard for Christians to say,

"God is my Father, and Jesus is my blood brother."

Jesus calls us brother, and we call Him Lord. At the same time we may just as well call Him brother, because He said he is not ashamed to call us His brethren.

There is one who holds faster than a brother, and that is a brother of covenant, a brother of blood. When two men are covenanted to one another, they are blood brothers. They are more like brothers than if they had been born from the same mother.

Jesus is your blood brother. You call Him Lord, because you serve Him; but He said, "if any man serve me, him will my Father honour" (John 12:26). God calls you His son. He wants to treat you like a king.

You may have been trying to sneak into the throne room of God, but He says, "Come boldly." If you start telling everyone how unworthy you are, there you go, dishonoring the sonship God has honored you with. Get rid of that attitude!

"But I'm bombarding the gates of heaven."

I don't know why. They aren't locked.

Quit storming the gates as though you can't get inside. Dare to come straight to the throne room. Enter it with a smile on your face, and say to the Lord, "I come boldly to present to You my needs, that I may obtain mercy and find grace to help in time of need."

If you will settle once and for all this question of

who you are in Christ Jesus, you will never have to
go another day without your needs being met fully
and abundantly.

Get in the Word of God and develop a firm faith
foundation. You will wake up one day and discover
those little things you were so worried about are all
yours—even the things you may have thought were a
little foolish. Your heavenly Father loves you, and He
wants you to have them.

Overtaken by Blessings

> And it shall come to pass, if thou shalt hear-
> ken diligently unto the voice of the Lord thy
> God, to observe and to do all his command-
> ments which I command thee this day, that the
> Lord thy God will set thee on high above all na-
> tions of the earth: And all these blessings shall
> come on thee, and overtake thee, if thou shalt
> hearken unto the voice of the Lord thy God
> (Deuteronomy 28:1-2).

A fellow came up to me one time and gave me something I was not asking the Lord for: a big car. I would
not have bought one like it if I had the money. I drive a
truck, not because I haul things, but because I like it.

I was surprised at what this man did. I said: "Lord, why did You give me a car like that? I never asked You for it. If I had the money I wouldn't have spent it on that. Why did You do that?"

He said: *Remember Deuteronomy 28? If you hearken diligently unto the voice of My Word and do what I ask you to do, all these blessings will come on you and overtake you. You just got overtaken!*

"That's just wonderful," I answered. "Do You want me to sell it?" It irritated Him when I said that.

No, I don't, He told me. *I thought you promised Me that if people gave money for something specific like the television ministry you wouldn't spend it on anything else.*

"That's right. I never have, and I never will."

Well, this man gave you that car to drive, didn't he? Not to sell it and put it into television. Why do you want to treat him like that?

"When am I going to wake up?" I asked.

When you quit being so traditional minded, He said. *Besides, I gave you that car because I appreciate some things you did for Me.*

I had never thought about that. It embarrassed me. I thought, *I wish I had done some more things I should have done!*

This just proves what we read in the Word, that acting on honor is thankworthy to God.

chapter 9

GOD CAN MAKE YOU HONORABLE

For years I lived outside any Christian influence other than the prayers of my mother and father. During that time I did everything I could to dodge a church service. The only time I would go was when my mother cornered me. Then when she got me in church, she would ask me to sing. For her sake I would do it. Then I would get out of there as fast as I could.

The night I was saved, I could tell that God or somebody like Him came into my room. My first thought was, *If I open my eyes, I'll see Jesus. And if I ever see Him, I'll have to preach.* So I kept my eyes closed.

Then I heard Jesus say deep down inside me, *If you don't get right with Me, you're going to a devil's hell.* I said, "I know it, Lord. What do I do now?"

Then I heard on the inside of me another voice. I recognized it. It was the Sunday school teacher I had when I was just a boy. Her name was Mrs. Taggert.

I thought she had probably been old all of her life, but all us boys loved her.

In the Southern Baptist church, children were promoted every year in Sunday school. We boys decided not to be promoted unless Mrs. Taggert could go along. We were determined that she was going to be our teacher, or we weren't going to move up. So she was promoted too. Mrs. Taggert had the same bunch of ornery boys for between three to five years. She was probably the only Sunday school teacher I ever had. Either that, or I don't remember the others because I didn't like them. But I sure liked her. Everybody did. Only we didn't call her Mrs. Taggert. We called her Old Lady Taggert—to her face— and she loved it (or at least she acted like she did).

Old Lady Taggert must have been 80 when she first started teaching us. She was so sweet, and she loved every one of us, but she could straighten us out fast. Nobody ever slept in her Sunday school class. She wore a little straw hat with a flower on the side of it, and everybody snapped to attention when Old Lady Taggert came into the room.

That night as an adult, I was sitting there saying, "God, I don't now what to do now." Right then I heard that familiar voice: *Boys, you have to ask Jesus to come into your hearts.*

I thought, *That's Old Lady Taggert!*

It was just as plain as if she had been in the room with me, even though she had long since gone home to be with the Lord. In that moment, the words she had spoken over and over to the boys in her Sunday school class came back to me.

Have you boys asked Jesus to come into your heart? Boys, you've got to ask Jesus to come into your heart.

She said it all the time.

The moment I heard her voice in my spirit that night, I acted on it. The Word she had taught us back when I was 12 years old became the foundation for my faith when I was born again.

Why didn't I get born again back when she told us that over and over?

I didn't pay any attention to it. I heard it. It went in me, but I never did act on it. I repented a lot, but it never occurred to me to make Jesus Lord of my life. I never even thought about it.

Baptists are big on salvation. They get more people born again than anybody. The Baptists get people saved.

I knew about that. We had lived in the shadow of Hardin-Simmons University in Abilene, Texas. It was second only to Baylor University in Waco, Texas, among Baptist schools, and my family went to the

University Baptist Church. Needless to say, I had heard the plan of salvation over and over again but it had never become the foundation for my faith.

Then when I heard the invitation that night— when I heard Old Lady Taggert say that I had to ask Jesus to come into my heart—I didn't wonder if He really would. I didn't hear it with my mind; it came up inside my spirit, and it seemed like the simplest thing I could ever do. So I asked Jesus to come into my heart. He did.

Actually, Mrs. Taggert won me to the Lord. God honored her witness to me 13 years before and the seed of her words sprang forth into eternal life inside me.

Honor Makes a Difference

There is a documentary about an abused child which I have seen twice. It is about a little girl who was abused by her parents. A pastor and his wife adopted her, not knowing the extent to which she had been abused by her biological parents. She was just a small child when the couple adopted her, but that little girl wanted to kill the whole family. She was asked about it:

"What were you trying to do to your brother

when your mother pulled you off him?"

"Kill him."

It didn't bother her at all to talk about it. The psychiatrist asked, "You mean you wanted to kill him?"

"Yeah."

"Were you hurting him?"

"Yeah."

"What were you doing to him?"

"Well, I had my hands on his throat, beating his head against the floor."

"Was your brother screaming for you to stop?"

"Yeah."

"But you wanted to kill him?"

"Yeah, I was gonna kill him."

"Why did you quit?"

"I heard Mama."

The girl showed no remorse whatsoever about what she had done. She had tried at one time or another to kill her whole family with some butcher knives.

"Where did you get the knives?" she was asked.

"Out of the dishwasher."

"What did you do with them?"

"I hid them."

This was an eight-year-old little girl. In school she had made it clear that she wanted to kill everybody in her class.

I want to inject this note. It will show you Satan's nature and what man is like when he is separated from the knowledge of God.

Satan is mean. He has death in him. Without a bonding to parents, many children wind up in the devil's clutches. The streets are full of them today. They don't care whether anyone else lives or dies. Why? Because their parents didn't care whether they lived or died. Their parents never bonded with them. They never taught them anything. They just threw them out with the garbage and let them grow up any way they could. Today we have an entire generation of godless people.

This little girl was placed in a home run by Christian people who knew how to treat this kind of child. There were some nine year olds in that same place who had committed murder, and didn't care. They were dangerous.

These adults begin to bond with the children. The youngsters couldn't do anything without adult supervision. They had to ask for every drink of water. If they didn't ask for it, they didn't get it. They had to get permission for everything they did. They were watched 24 hours a day. They had alarms on their doors. They couldn't move at night without somebody being there to watch them.

The counselors were constantly working with these children, telling them over and over again, "God loves you, and I love you."

A year or two after the little girl was sent to this place, she was interviewed again and asked the same questions. This time she was holding a little white Bible in her hand, and she was so proud of it.

"What were you trying to do when you were hurting your brother?" she was asked.

"It was trying to kill him," she answered. But this time, she started weeping and couldn't talk about it.

What had happened to make such a change in her? She had been born again. She had become honorable toward her brother, her parents and God.

God Can Make Us Honorable

God can make us honorable. He honors us with His own life. What the Bible calls eternal life is administered to our spirit man by the Holy Spirit. Then He instills in us the desire to honor Him in how we conduct our lives.

When I was born again, I was suddenly filled with the desire to honor God. When the little girl who had tried to kill her family was born again, she was filled with the desire to honor God and obey Him, even to the extent of honoring her family.

God wants us honorable. If you are not honorable, now is the time to go before the Father and ask Him to make you that way.

Satan Will Try to Steal This Word

The sower soweth the word. And these are they by the way side, where the word is sown; but when they have heard, Satan cometh immediately, and taketh away the word that was sown in their hearts. And these are they likewise which are sown on stony ground; who, when they have heard the word, immediately receive it with gladness; and have no root in themselves, and so endure but for a time: afterward, when affliction or persecution ariseth for the word's sake, immediately they are offended. And these are they which are sown among thorns; such as hear the word, and the cares of this world, and the deceitfulness of riches, and the lusts of other things entering in, choke the word, and it becometh unfruitful. And these are they which are sown on good ground; such as hear the word, and receive it, and bring forth fruit, some thirtyfold, some sixty, and some an hundred (Mark 4:14-20).

You must realize that honor is a powerful spiritual force, and Satan will try to keep you from walking in it. He will try to steal this word. I want you to know what he is going to use against you to do it. You don't have to fall for his devices. Greater is He who is in us than he who is in the world (1 John 4:4)!

In the parable of the sower and the seed, Jesus warned that, when the sower sows the Word, the devil comes immediately to steal it from those who have heard and received it.

He did not bother to talk about those who refused to receive the Word. What was there to say about them? Nothing. He talked about those who did receive it.

They received it gladly, but some did not hold onto it long. Many allowed the devil to steal it for one reason or another. Some let him steal all of it. Others let him steal fortyfold, and they only retained sixtyfold. Still others did not let him have any of it.

You can depend on the fact that Satan will try to steal the Word out of your heart. You need to study those areas of the Word, particularly Mark 4, to learn how your enemy operates. He only has five ways to attack you. Read this passage again carefully to find out what they are. Make the decision to resist the devil and his devices, then stand firm on your decision.

Hear and Receive

If any man have ears to hear, let him hear. And he said unto them, Take heed what ye hear: with what measure ye mete, it shall be measured to you: and unto you that hear shall more be given. For he that hath, to him shall be given: and he that hath not, from him shall be taken even that which he hath (Mark 4:23-25).

After explaining the meaning of the parable, Jesus told His disciples, "Be careful how you hear, because that will determine how you receive."

He went on to say something startling: "Those who have will receive more." Have what? Ears that take heed to what they hear. "And those who have not ears that take heed to what they hear are going to lose what little they do have." Satan will come and steal it.

A Firm Faith Foundation

These biblical laws that I have shared with you

from God's Word will help you in building a firm foundation of faith.

Go over them again and again. Stay with them. Learn from them. They are food to your spirit. Renew your mind with God's Word, particularly the financial truths of God's Word, because we are combating traditions that, in some cases, are over 1,000 years old.

As somebody said, "Grandma taught it, and we bought it." Grandma did not mean to tell us something wrong; she was only passing along what she had heard. Each generation before us had less revelation than this generation does today.

Each generation, according to God's plan, should grow in revelation. Each generation should pass on what it knows. The next generation should grow in God and add to that body of knowledge. This is especially true in regard to what the Word has to say about material prosperity.

I can be reading along in the Scriptures, see something and think, *Why didn't I see that before?* The Lord will say, *Because of your religious tradition.* Such traditional ideas have robbed us over the years. As we progress, we hear God saying new and different things—exciting things that we never heard before.

We have been locked up in the capsule of these pages together, studying biblical honor. It has been informative and inspiring. But soon we will go back into the real world, out where Satan tries to attack and destroy.

Stay before God. Do as James said: Keep your tongue under control and don't lie against the truth (James 3:2-14). If you don't know what the truth is, say nothing one way or the other. Just be quiet. Say, "Lord, give me the answer to this situation; I believe I receive it."

Don't worry about what other people think or say or do. We all are different and have different convictions, understandings and interpretations. Just walk in faith and in love. Don't criticize anybody. Keep listening, reading, walking, loving and believing. The Spirit of truth will lead you into all truth.

Come, Hear, Do

A good man out of the good treasure of his heart bringeth forth that which is good; and an evil man out of the evil treasure of his heart bringeth forth that which is evil: for of the abundance of the heart his mouth speaketh. And why call ye me, Lord, Lord, and do not the things which I say? Whosoever cometh to me, and heareth my sayings, and doeth them, I will show you to whom he is like (Luke 6:45-47).

Whosoever cometh to me.... Come to Him. Don't pay attention to everybody in the whole world and everything they say. Come to Jesus. He's your Lord.

...and heareth my sayings.... Come to Him and hear His Word. Have faith in the Living Word, Jesus.

...and doeth them.... Come to Him, hear His Word and do it. Be a doer of the Word and not a hearer only (James 1:22).

...I will show you to whom he is like. What is the person like who does these three important things? Let's look further in God's Word.

Founded Upon a Rock

He is like a man which built an house, and digged deep, and laid the foundation on a rock: and when the flood arose, the stream beat vehemently upon that house, and could not shake it: for it was founded upon a rock (Luke 6:48).

"For it was founded upon a rock." Read this phrase out loud: "For it was founded upon a *rock*." That is the firm faith foundation each of us needs in our lives. We develop that foundation by coming to Jesus, hearing His Word and doing it.

The House Without Foundation

> But he that heareth, and doeth not, is like a man that without a foundation built an house upon the earth; against which the stream did beat vehemently, and immediately it fell; and the ruin of that house was great (Luke 6:49).

Notice that the storm hit both houses. It was not the storm that destroyed the house. If the storm had the power to destroy all houses, it would have destroyed both of them; but it did not.

But rather, the lack of foundation destroyed one house. The firm foundation saved the other. That foundation was hearing and doing. Allow what you hear from God's Word to become the determining factor in what you do.

Jesus, the Living Word

> For the word of God is quick [alive], and powerful, and sharper than any twoedged sword, piercing even to the dividing asunder of soul

and spirit, and of the joints and marrow, and is a discerner of the thoughts and intents of the heart. Neither is there any creature that is not manifest in his sight: but all things are naked and opened unto the eyes of him with whom we have to do (Hebrews 4:12-13).

Is Jesus the Word of God? Yes, He is. This scripture says that the Word is alive. The living Word is the foundation of our faith.

Without the Word of God in us, even though we may be doing all the right works and saying all the right things, we have no foundation for any of it.

There have been people over the years who have tried to walk on my faith. They did what I did and said what I said. Then when the storm hit, I didn't fall, but they did—and they got mad at me!

I wasn't the one who knocked their foundation out from under them. They never really had a foundation. They had listened to tapes, read books and followed many religious exercises. But when the storm came, instead of standing on God's Word, they backed away and said, "What Kenneth Copeland said doesn't work." That's the problem. Kenneth Copeland didn't say it. God said it. It's the Word that will never pass away.

Word and Spirit

It is the spirit that quickeneth [makes alive]; the flesh profiteth nothing: the words that I speak unto you, they are spirit, and they are life (John 6:63).

What man says doesn't really mean a thing in and of itself. What I say will not necessarily stand up—unless what I say is based on the Word of God.

I say that I am healed, regardless of the condition of my body. I say that as a praise to God because my body is well, or as a confession of faith to change my body if it is not well. In either case, all I am going to say is that I am healed. I am not speaking from my position in my body; I am speaking from my position in Christ Jesus.

There are all kinds of misunderstandings about this principle. The reason I say I am healed is not because I heard some great man of God say it. I say I am healed because I learned it from God's Word. I stayed in the Word until it came alive in my spirit and rose up in my mouth. That is more real to me than the symptoms in my body.

I don't go around saying I am healed just because

I am part of the "faith movement." If that were the case, the first time anything went wrong with my body my confession would crumble and fall apart. I say I am healed because the living Word is the foundation of my faith.

The Word lies dormant in a person's life until it becomes the foundation for his faith. Some people can quote much of the Bible, but it is not the foundation for their faith. Actually what they are doing is confessing, but their confession is coming out of the mind instead of the spirit. The power is not in the flesh, but in the spirit: the re-created human spirit, the Holy Spirit, the spirit realm.

The Foundation of Revelation Knowledge

When Jesus came into the coasts of Caesarea Philippi, he asked his disciples, saying, Whom do men say that I the Son of man am? And they said, Some say that thou art John the Baptist: some, Elias; and others, Jeremias, or one of the prophets. He saith unto them, But whom say ye that I am? And Simon Peter answered and said, Thou art the Christ, the Son of the living God. And Jesus answered and said unto him, Blessed art thou, Simon Bar-jona: for flesh and

blood hath not revealed it unto thee, but my
Father which is in heaven. And I say also unto
thee, That thou art Peter, and upon this rock I
will build my church; and the gates of hell shall
not prevail against it (Matthew 16:13-18).

Jesus is not talking about building His Church
on Peter. There have been all kinds of controversies
about this. But that is not what He was talking about.
When Jesus said this He was using two different
genders. He used the masculine gender in one and
the feminine gender in the other. So he couldn't have
been referring to Peter both times.

He told Peter, "This truth has not come to you
from flesh and blood, but from My Father in heaven."
What did Peter receive? A revelation from God—a
spiritual revelation. That did not come through his
eyes or his ears or any of his physical senses. It came
from his spirit into his mind.

Jesus said to Peter: "Your physical senses did not
reveal this truth to you. My heavenly Father revealed
it to you. Because of this revelation, you are a rock.
You have a foundation."

In another incident He told Martha that Mary
sat at His feet, heard His Word and chose that good
thing which nobody could take away from her

(Luke 10:40-42). What was it? The Word of God.

A revelation of God's Word comes from your spirit into your consciousness. No human being on earth can take that away from you. Only you can turn it loose or ignore it until it becomes inoperative in your life.

It will lie there dormant until once again it becomes the foundation for your faith. If you stir it up, the seed will germinate again. It will come alive.

Jesus told Peter: "You are a rock, because what you have received is a revelation from God. I will build My Church on that rock—the foundation of revelation knowledge—and the gates of hell will not prevail against it."

Living in the Spirit Realm

And I will give unto thee the keys of the kingdom of heaven: and whatsoever thou shalt bind on earth shall be bound in heaven: and whatsoever thou shalt loose on earth shall be loosed in heaven (Matthew 16:19).

This familiar passage on the keys of heaven and binding and loosing brings up some interesting questions: What is the realm of faith like? Why should we be so vitally, constantly, continually interested in faith?

Think about how we protect the feeding of our physical bodies. We may claim that we have no time to spend in the Word of God, but we don't miss any meals! There is no such thing as not having time to eat—not for long. The same should be true of our spiritual nourishment.

We must do something about this attitude, especially as we move forward toward the catching away of the Church. The Church that has already gone to heaven and the Church that is still on earth are going to meet one day and never be separated again. The Bible says that one day we will be like our Lord and Savior Jesus Christ (1 John 3:2).

The closer we get to that day, the more is required of us. As the time grows shorter and shorter, the more we in the Church are going to have to learn more and more how to schedule our work time around the Word instead of trying to schedule the Word around our work time.

This is not something we *ought* to do. It is something we *must* do. If we do it, there will be more revelation poured out on the Body of Christ than there has been in the past 2,000 years combined. We will be either the most spiritually knowledgeable or the most spiritually ignorant generation in history.

The faith realm must come first, because faith is the catalyst that hooks the natural world and the spiritual world together. We cannot get from one to the other without the spiritual force of faith.

The Bible says to be carnally minded (in debt to the flesh) is death, but to be spiritually minded (free from debt to the flesh) is life (Romans 8:4-13). If we are operating in the realm of the spirit, there is no way the flesh can dominate us, because we will be dominating it. That truth is so vital in the day in which we live.

Hold Fast to Faith

Wherefore seeing we also are compassed about with so great a cloud of witnesses, let us lay aside every weight, and the sin which doth so easily beset us, and let us run with patience the race that is set before us, looking unto Jesus the author and finisher of our faith...(Hebrews 12:1-2).

Faith holds fast to its foundation. What is the foundation of faith? The living Word.

We must be honest with ourselves. We are dealing with life and death. We must not be artificial. As one fellow said about Hollywood, "Under that phony tinsel is some real tinsel." Sadly enough, there are many people in the Body of Christ who are like that; they are totally unreal. The way we become real is first by being honest with ourselves and second, by getting honest with God.

Not only is the living Word the foundation of faith, but faith holds fast to the Word. So then faith cometh by hearing, and hearing by the word of God (Romans 10:17). I like what Brother Kenneth Hagin says about this verse: "It doesn't say that faith comes by having heard; it says that faith comes by hearing, and hearing, and hearing."

The time is fast approaching when we are going to need our faith. Why? Because trouble is coming.

"But, Brother Copeland, I thought you were a victory preacher."

I am. What do you think we get victory over? One another? No, over trouble, over trial and tribulation. There have not been any "good old days" since the Garden of Eden. There are not any good times—except for those who believe their way into good times.

Let's Be Honorable!

Be not slothful, but followers of them who through faith and patience inherit the promises (Hebrews 6:12).

God has honored us with great power and authority.

Jesus paid us the greatest honor by going to the cross for us, shedding His blood and paying the price for our sins. We are crowned with glory and honor. The Lord honors us with His Name, and all authority is given unto us. He honors our faith. He honors His Word, and He honors the Word that is active and alive in us. He honors us with answered prayer. Thank God, He honors us!

We can honor Him with our obedience, our praise, our very lives as they are offered up as a living sacrifice unto Him. It is a joy to honor our God.

He wants us to be honorable before Him.

God is calling us to be accountable to Him in this crucial hour—totally, completely honest and real before Him. He wants us to be honorable to each other, honorable in our business dealings and honorable in the eyes of the world. The eyes of the world are on the Body of Christ as never before. The world is watching as God pours out His power upon us.

Let's be vessels of honor. Let's not hinder the greatest outpouring of the supernatural power of God in history in these last days. Let's walk in honor, moving along step by step with the Spirit of the Lord as He takes us closer and closer toward the climax of the ages—the return of Jesus Christ.

Do what's right.
Do it because it's right, then...
Do it right.

Prayer for Salvation and Baptism
in the Holy Spirit

Heavenly Father, I come to You in the Name of Jesus. Your Word says, "Whosoever shall call on the name of the Lord shall be saved" (Acts 2:21). I am calling on You. I pray and ask Jesus to come into my heart and be Lord over my life according to Romans 10:9-10: "If thou shalt confess with thy mouth the Lord Jesus, and shalt believe in thine heart that God hath raised him from the dead, thou shalt be saved. For with the heart man believeth unto righteousness; and with the mouth confession is made unto salvation." I do that now. I confess that Jesus is Lord, and I believe in my heart that God raised Him from the dead. I repent of sin. I renounce it. I renounce the devil and everything he stands for. Jesus is my Lord.

I am now reborn! I am a Christian—a child of Almighty God! I am saved! You also said in Your Word, "If ye then, being evil, know how to give good gifts unto your children: HOW MUCH MORE shall your heavenly Father give the Holy Spirit to them that ask him?" (Luke 11:13). I'm also asking You to fill me with the Holy Spirit. Holy Spirit, rise up within me as I praise God. I fully expect to speak with other tongues as You give me the utterance (Acts 2:4). In Jesus' Name. Amen!

Begin to praise God for filling you with the Holy Spirit. Speak those words and syllables you receive—not in your own language, but the language given to you by the Holy Spirit. You have to use your own voice. God will not force you to speak. Don't be concerned with how it sounds. It is a heavenly language!

Continue with the blessing God has given you and pray in the spirit every day.

You are a born-again, Spirit-filled believer. You'll never be the same!

Find a good church that boldly preaches God's Word and obeys it. Become part of a church family who will love and care for you as you love and care for them.

We need to be connected to each other. It increases our strength in God. It's God's plan for us.

Make it a habit to watch the Believer's Voice of Victory Network and become a doer of the Word, who is blessed in his doing (James 1:22-25).

About the Author

Kenneth Copeland is co-founder and president of Kenneth Copeland Ministries in Fort Worth, Texas, and best-selling author of books that include *Honor—Walking in Honesty, Truth and Integrity,* and *THE BLESSING of The LORD Makes Rich and He Adds No Sorrow With It.*

Since 1967, Kenneth has been a minister of the gospel of Christ and teacher of God's Word. He is also the artist on award-winning albums such as his Grammy-nominated *Only the Redeemed, In His Presence, He Is Jehovah, Just a Closer Walk* and *Big Band Gospel.* He also co-stars as the character Wichita Slim in the children's adventure videos *The Gunslinger, Covenant Rider* and the movie *The Treasure of Eagle Mountain,* and as Daniel Lyon in the Commander Kellie and the Superkids™ videos *Armor of Light* and *Judgment: The Trial of Commander Kellie.* Kenneth also co-stars as a Hispanic godfather in the 2009 and 2016 movies *The Rally* and *The Rally 2: Breaking the Curse.*

With the help of offices and staff in the United States, Canada, England, Australia, South Africa and Ukraine, Kenneth is fulfilling his vision to boldly preach the uncompromised WORD of God from the top of this world, to the bottom, and all the way around. His ministry reaches millions of people worldwide through daily and Sunday TV broadcasts, magazines, teaching audios and videos, conventions and campaigns, and the World Wide Web.

When The LORD first spoke to Kenneth and Gloria Copeland about starting the *Believer's Voice of Victory* magazine...

He said: This is your seed. Give it to everyone who ever responds to your ministry, and don't ever allow anyone to pay for a subscription!

For more than 50 years, it has been the joy of Kenneth Copeland Ministries to bring the good news to believers. Readers enjoy teaching from ministers who write from lives of living contact with God, and testimonies from believers experiencing victory through God's WORD in their everyday lives.

Today, the *BVOV* magazine is mailed monthly, bringing encouragement and blessing to believers around the world. Many even use it as a ministry tool, passing it on to others who desire to know Jesus and grow in their faith!

Request your FREE subscription to the
Believer's Voice of Victory magazine today!

Go to **freevictory.com** to subscribe online, or call us at
1-800-600-7395 (U.S. only) or **+1-817-852-6000**.

We're Here for You!®

Your growth in God's WORD and victory in Jesus are at the very center of our hearts. In every way God has equipped us, we will help you deal with the issues facing you, so you can be the **victorious overcomer** He has planned for you to be.

The mission of Kenneth Copeland Ministries is about all of us growing and going together. Our prayer is that you will take full advantage of all The LORD has given us to share with you.

Wherever you are in the world, you can watch the *Believer's Voice of Victory* broadcast on television (check your local listings), the Internet at kcm.org or on our digital Roku channel.

Our website, **kcm.org,** gives you access to every resource we've developed for your victory. And, you can find contact information for our international offices in Africa, Australia, Canada, Europe, Ukraine and our headquarters in the United States.

Each office is staffed with devoted men and women, ready to serve and pray with you. You can contact the worldwide office nearest you for assistance, and you can call us for prayer at our U.S. number, +1-817-852-6000, 24 hours every day!

We encourage you to connect with us often and let us be part of your everyday walk of faith!

Jesus Is LORD!

Kenneth & Gloria Copeland

Kenneth and Gloria Copeland